A Self Help Book For Depression

CRAFTED BY SKRIUWER

Copyright © 2024 by Skriuwer.

All rights reserved. No part of this book may be used or reproduced in any form whatsoever without written permission except in the case of brief quotations in critical articles or reviews.

For more information, contact : **kontakt@skriuwer.com** (www.skriuwer.com)

TABLE OF CONTENTS

CHAPTER 1: UNDERSTANDING DEPRESSION

- Explains what depression is and how it can affect your daily life
- Discusses possible causes and factors linked to depression
- Identifies common signs to watch for

CHAPTER 2: BREAKING MYTHS

- Clarifies false beliefs about depression
- Shares facts to correct unhelpful ideas
- Encourages a more understanding view of mental health

CHAPTER 3: NOTING COMMON SIGNS

- Shows different ways depression can appear
- Points out emotional, physical, and behavioral clues
- Helps you spot early warning signals

CHAPTER 4: BUILDING HELPFUL RELATIONSHIPS

- Highlights the power of human connection
- Suggests ways to find and maintain supportive bonds
- Addresses handling unhelpful or toxic ties

CHAPTER 5: USING HEALTHY ROUTINES

- Describes how stable daily habits support mood
- Gives tips on small steps to form lasting routines
- Shows how structure can reduce stress

CHAPTER 6: EATING WELL

- *Explains how food choices can influence your emotions*
- *Offers practical ways to adopt healthier eating patterns*
- *Suggests easy meal ideas and mindful eating tips*

CHAPTER 7: STAYING PHYSICALLY ACTIVE

- *Reveals how gentle movement can lift mood and energy*
- *Presents simple activity ideas for all ability levels*
- *Gives methods for overcoming low motivation*

CHAPTER 8: QUIETING THE MIND

- *Explores methods to reduce mental noise*
- *Teaches breathing and relaxation exercises*
- *Provides ways to find small moments of calm*

CHAPTER 9: SHIFTING NEGATIVE THOUGHTS

- *Covers how to recognize harmful thinking patterns*
- *Shares techniques to replace dark ideas with balanced ones*
- *Introduces ways to question and alter self-talk*

CHAPTER 10: PLANNING TASKS

- *Details how to make tasks and chores feel manageable*
- *Suggests breaking big goals into smaller steps*
- *Explains how to organize time and avoid overwhelm*

CHAPTER 11: IMPROVING SLEEP

- *Shows why rest matters and how it impacts mood*
- *Offers tips for making bedtime calm and stable*
- *Talks about handling worries and night-time tension*

CHAPTER 12: EASING TENSION

- Discusses how stress builds up in mind and body
- Shares techniques to relax muscles and release anxiety
- Explains how small breaks can prevent overwhelm

CHAPTER 13: ARTS AND EXPRESSION

- Highlights creativity as a way to release deep feelings
- Suggests drawing, writing, music, or dance for relief
- Encourages safe self-expression without judgment

CHAPTER 14: SEEING YOURSELF KINDLY

- Focuses on self-compassion and countering harsh inner talk
- Shows how to handle self-blame and low self-esteem
- Promotes a fair, gentle view of personal worth

CHAPTER 15: HANDLING GUILT

- Differentiates between helpful and harmful guilt
- Gives steps for apologizing, making amends, and moving on
- Encourages self-forgiveness and balanced responsibility

CHAPTER 16: SPEAKING UP AND CREATING LIMITS

- Explains how to set boundaries for healthier relationships
- Teaches ways to say "no" and stand up for your needs
- Describes avoiding guilt while protecting your well-being

CHAPTER 17: PROFESSIONAL SUPPORT

- Describes types of counselors, psychologists, and psychiatrists
- Explains what to expect in therapy or when seeking help
- Talks about medication, costs, and finding the right match

CHAPTER 18: CHECKING PROGRESS

- *Explores methods for tracking mood and daily habits*
- *Helps you notice slow changes and handle setbacks*
- *Shows how to adjust your strategies based on patterns*

CHAPTER 19: KEEPING STEADY GAINS

- *Reveals ways to maintain positive changes over time*
- *Addresses preventing relapses and using coping tools*
- *Advises on refining routines and emotional stability*

CHAPTER 20: HOPE FOR THE FUTURE

- *Centers on building a sense of hope beyond depression*
- *Suggests looking ahead with realistic optimism*
- *Shows how to find purpose and hold onto brighter possibilities*

Chapter 1: Understanding Depression

Depression is a strong and deep sadness that does not go away quickly. It can affect people of any age, including children. It can feel like a heavy weight that makes it hard to get out of bed or do things you once liked. You might feel alone and tired. You might feel hopeless. Even if people around you say kind words or offer support, those feelings may still remain. This chapter will explain what depression is, why it happens, and how it can make you think or act in certain ways.

What Is Depression?

Depression is a mental health concern. It can make you feel sad, helpless, and unable to do daily tasks. Sometimes, you do not want to be around friends and family. You might feel weak, as if you have no energy. It can also affect your physical health. You might have headaches or an upset stomach. You might feel pain in your muscles. Depression is more than normal sadness. Sometimes, sadness is a reaction to a hard event, like losing a pet or having a fight with a loved one. But depression can stay even when things around you improve.

When you experience this condition, your view of the world might become darker. Small tasks can feel huge. Activities you once found fun no longer give you any feeling of joy. You might lose your appetite. You might start sleeping too much or not being able to sleep at all. Depression can also change how you think about yourself. You could have negative thoughts that say you are not good enough. You might think you have failed or let others down, even if that is not true.

Possible Causes

Many factors can play a role in bringing on depression. These factors can include your body and your mind. Let us look at a few possible causes:

1. **Genetics**: Depression can run in families. If one or both of your parents, or close relatives, have felt depressed, you may have a higher chance of experiencing it. This does not mean you will have depression for sure, but the odds may be higher.
2. **Brain Chemistry**: Sometimes, the brain's chemicals can be off balance. These chemicals are like messengers that pass signals from one brain cell to another. They help control mood, thoughts, and feelings. If these chemicals are not balanced, it can lead to low mood and sadness that lasts for a long time.
3. **Life Events**: Hard or stressful events can lead to depression. Examples could be problems at home, like parents arguing. It could also be losing a friend or moving to a new town. Even changing schools can be stressful. These problems can make you feel alone or worried. Sometimes, if you already have a tendency for depression, these events can set it off.
4. **Health Issues**: If you have a serious illness or injury, you might start to feel sad and empty. Long-term health problems can put a strain on both your mind and body. Feeling pain, going to the hospital often, or missing out on social activities can add to sadness.
5. **Negative Thinking Patterns**: Some people tend to think badly about themselves and their lives. These thoughts might happen often. Over time, this pattern can make you feel hopeless or ashamed.

Signs You Might Notice

You might ask yourself, "How do I know if I or someone I care about is depressed?" While there is no single sign that applies to everyone, there are common clues:

- **Persistent Sadness**: Feeling sad or down most days, for many hours of the day.
- **Lack of Interest**: No desire to do activities you once liked, such as playing games, drawing, or talking with friends.
- **Changes in Eating**: Eating much more or much less than usual. This might cause weight gain or weight loss.
- **Changes in Sleep**: Sleeping too much or not sleeping enough. You might wake up many times at night or find it difficult to fall asleep.
- **Feeling Tired**: Feeling drained even when you have not done much. You might find it hard to get up in the morning.
- **Guilt or Worthlessness**: Thinking you have no value. Blaming yourself for things you have no control over.
- **Trouble Concentrating**: Having a hard time focusing on schoolwork, reading, or watching a show. You might feel your mind is foggy.
- **Moving Slowly or Feeling Restless**: You could feel you are moving and speaking more slowly than before. Or you might not be able to sit still and feel on edge all day.
- **Dark or Hopeless Thoughts**: You might feel life is pointless. In some cases, people have thoughts of harming themselves or ending their lives.

Differences Among People

Depression does not look the same in everyone. One person might feel hopeless and tearful all day. Another person might seem angry or cranky. Sometimes, younger folks become more withdrawn, not wanting to be around others. Teens might act out or get into trouble at school. Adults might become quiet or show signs of stress at work.

There is not one single correct way to feel depressed. Some people hide their sadness very well and still look happy to others. Others might cry or stay in bed all day. All these forms of depression deserve equal care. Each person's experience is real.

How Depression Can Affect Daily Life

When you are depressed, even simple tasks can feel large. Things like cleaning your room or taking a bath might feel like big chores. Schoolwork can be harder because you cannot focus. Tests and assignments might become scary. You might worry about failing, which can feed negative thoughts about yourself.

You might withdraw from friends and family. You could stop going to events or clubs. This can make you feel even more alone. Depression can make you believe that nobody understands you. It can cause arguments with loved ones. They might not grasp why you are acting differently. If you feel misunderstood, you might become frustrated or sadder.

Over time, these effects can form a cycle. You feel bad, so you withdraw. That leads to fewer positive experiences. This can confirm your negative thoughts, making you feel worse. It can be difficult to break out of this pattern.

The Importance of Recognizing Depression

Identifying depression early is helpful. If you sense you might be depressed, reaching out to a trusted adult, friend, or counselor can be a first step. Sometimes, just talking about it can provide a small sense of ease. Talking about how you feel helps you understand that you are not alone. You might see that others have gone through something similar. This knowledge can encourage you to seek support.

Depression is more common than people think. Many people suffer in silence because they feel weak or ashamed. But seeking help is not weak. It is a step toward feeling better.

Ways People Can Begin to Address Depression

1. **Talking to Someone**: Sharing feelings with a friend, family member, or mental health professional can help. Sometimes, others can provide a new point of view. They can also offer helpful ideas you did not consider.
2. **Writing in a Journal**: Some find it helpful to write down thoughts when they are feeling low. A journal can serve as a safe space to be honest about your emotions.
3. **Trying Activities That Soothe**: Some people find comfort in music, reading, or drawing. These activities can calm the mind and reduce stress. They may not remove all sadness, but they can bring moments of calm.
4. **Looking at Sleep Habits**: Your sleep schedule affects your mood. If you do not get enough rest, your sadness can grow. Sticking to a regular bedtime can help.
5. **Deep Breathing**: Taking slow breaths can calm your nervous system. Even a few moments of mindful breathing can help you feel more settled.
6. **Professional Support**: Counselors, psychologists, or psychiatrists are trained to help you. They can show you tools to handle negative thoughts. They can give advice on small steps to feel better.

What Depression Is Not

Depression is not a sign that you are a bad person. It is not something you can simply wish away. It is not a sign of being lazy. Depression is also not just "feeling sad" for a day or two. While everyday sadness is normal, depression lasts longer and affects how you function.

Depression does not define who you are. You are not "broken." Many people have felt hopeless at some point and have found relief with support, time, and the right tools.

The Stigma Around Depression

A stigma is a negative label that people place on something they do not understand well. Sometimes, people judge those with depression. They might think it is a made-up issue. They might say, "Snap out of it," or, "You have nothing to be sad about." These statements are not helpful because depression goes beyond temporary sadness.

This stigma can prevent many from asking for help. They might fear being called weak. But talking about mental health in a caring way can help reduce this stigma. Remember, depression is a recognized condition that affects millions. It requires care just like any physical illness does.

Finding Comfort in Understanding

Once you know more about depression, it becomes less scary. You realize it is not your fault that you feel this way. You also learn that there are steps to deal with it. You can talk to a friend or family member, visit a mental health professional, or make changes in your everyday life that might help.

Knowledge can bring a sense of relief. When you see that depression is a condition with known patterns and possible responses, you can feel a bit more in control. You begin to see that you are not alone in this.

The Role of Openness

Being open about how you feel can be difficult at first. You might worry that others will not listen or might judge you. But sharing your thoughts, even in a simple way, can remove some of the burden you carry inside. You might find comfort in having someone say, "I understand" or "I care." You can also ask for specific help, such as, "Can we talk for a few minutes every day?" or, "Could you help me with this task that feels overwhelming?"

When others know you are feeling down, they can offer patience and support. They might check on you more often. They might share resources, like support groups. These small acts can help lighten your load.

Setting the Stage for Getting Better

Learning about depression is a strong first step. It helps you see that you are dealing with a real concern. It also shows that there are many things you can do. In later chapters, we will discuss more tools and ideas to help you. You will learn about healthy routines, physical activity, better sleep, and seeking professional help. Each piece of information will support you in different ways. Over time, using more than one tool can offer relief and help you feel more stable.

Everyone has a different starting point. Some have access to a strong support system, like close friends and caring family. Others might not have many people they can turn to. But even if you feel alone, there are phone hotlines, mental health websites, and community centers that can help. Do not give up if the first person you turn to does not understand. Keep seeking someone who will listen.

Why Each Step Matters

Depression can make you feel that nothing matters. You might think no step is worth the effort. But small steps do matter, even if they do not solve everything at once. Feeling a bit better for a short time can pave the way for feeling better again. Each small bit of relief can encourage you to keep going. Even something as simple as sharing your worries can be a sign of progress.

You might need many kinds of help at once. For example, talking to a counselor while also working on improving your sleep can produce better results than just one of those steps alone. Depression is serious, and many times, it will require a combination of approaches.

Looking Ahead

This first chapter gave a broad view of what depression is. We discussed how it can make you feel, what might cause it, and why it is important to understand it. If you feel depressed or suspect someone close to you is depressed, remember that knowledge is the first step toward relief. You do not have to face this alone. There are people and resources that can help you find ways to handle it.

Chapter 2: Breaking Myths

False ideas about depression can create barriers for those who need help. Myths can make people feel ashamed or afraid to speak up. They might think depression is a sign of weakness, or that only certain kinds of people get depressed. These untrue ideas can also cause family and friends to judge or misunderstand a person who is depressed. In this chapter, we will discuss common myths and offer facts to replace them.

Myth 1: "Depression Is Not Real"

Some people believe depression is made up. They might say it is just a bad mood or a way to get attention. In reality, depression is recognized by doctors and mental health professionals around the world. It is a condition that affects the brain and the body. Brain scans and other studies show changes in brain activity in those with depression. You cannot simply decide not to feel depressed, just like you cannot wish away a broken bone.

Fact: Depression is real and has many causes, including changes in brain chemistry, life events, and genetics.

Myth 2: "Only Adults Get Depressed"

Many think depression only affects grown-ups who have jobs, bills, and responsibilities. But children and teenagers can also feel depressed. They can face stress at school, bullying, family conflicts, or worries about the future. Younger individuals might not know how to express their sadness. They might act out in class or withdraw from activities. Their depression is just as real as an adult's.

Fact: Young people can experience depression too. They might show it in different ways, but it is still serious.

Myth 3: "You Can Snap Out of It"

A common false idea is that if you try hard enough, you can stop feeling depressed by sheer willpower. People might say, "Think positively," or, "Stop being sad." If it were that simple, few people would struggle with depression. While positive thinking can help to a small extent, depression often demands more than just a change in attitude. It might involve therapy, medication, or other long-term changes in your life.

Fact: Depression usually needs professional support, lifestyle changes, or both. It is not a sign of laziness or lack of willpower.

Myth 4: "Depression Is Always Caused by a Big Event"

Some assume you can only become depressed if you face a major crisis, like losing a family member. While that can be a trigger for depression, not everyone with depression has gone through a huge event. Sometimes depression appears without a clear reason. It might be related to genetics or chemical changes in the brain. So if your life seems normal on the outside, you could still feel depressed.

Fact: Depression can happen to anyone, at any time, even if things look fine from the outside.

Myth 5: "People With Depression Are Always Sad"

When you think of depression, you might picture someone crying often or lying in bed all day. While these are common signs, depression can show up in many ways. Some people become very irritable. Others feel numb, as if they have no emotions. Some still go to school or work every day but feel hollow inside. They might force a smile to hide their true feelings. Depression does not have to be obvious to be real.

Fact: Depression can cause many different moods, including anger, numbness, or sadness.

Myth 6: "Medication Fixes Everything"

Medication can help rebalance chemicals in the brain. This can ease some symptoms of depression. However, medication alone might not fix deeper problems, like negative thinking patterns or harmful habits. Therapy, healthy relationships, and stable daily routines are also important. Many people find the best approach is to use both medication (if needed) and regular therapy sessions. Others do well with therapy alone. The right approach depends on each person's situation.

Fact: Medication is only one piece of the puzzle. Careful planning often involves several different methods.

Myth 7: "Talking About Depression Makes It Worse"

Some worry that talking about sad thoughts will make them grow. They might think it is better to ignore those feelings or keep them hidden. The truth is, sharing emotions with a trusted friend, family member, or counselor can help you sort out your thoughts. It can lessen shame and help you see things more clearly. Bottling up feelings often makes them heavier in the long run.

Fact: Open talks about depression can help ease heavy emotions and encourage steps toward help.

Myth 8: "People With Depression Are Weak"

A harmful falsehood is that depressed individuals are not strong or cannot handle life's problems. In fact, many people with depression handle large challenges every day. They get out of bed even when it feels impossible. They try their best at school or work. Dealing with depression often requires courage and strength. It takes a lot of effort to keep going while feeling so low.

Fact: Having depression does not mean you are weak. It is an illness that can happen to the strongest of people.

Myth 9: "Depression Is the Same for Everyone"

You might see a movie or show where a character with depression looks a certain way. They might cry a lot or talk in a monotone voice. This can make you think everyone with depression must show the same signs. But mental health concerns vary from person to person. One person might lose their appetite, while another might eat more. One might feel fearful, while another might be numb. Different people have different ways of coping.

Fact: Each person's depression can feel different, and symptoms can change over time.

Myth 10: "Seeking Help Means You Are Giving Up"

It can be hard to admit you need help. Some people fear that going to a therapist or taking medication means they have failed. But seeking help is actually an active step. It shows that you are trying to feel better. Recognizing you need support is not giving up. Instead, it is one of the bravest actions you can take for your well-being.

Fact: Asking for support is a sign of responsibility and strength, not surrender.

How Myths Can Harm People

These untrue ideas often make it harder for people to speak about their depression or look for treatment. They might stay silent out of shame or fear. Friends or family who believe these myths might not offer proper understanding or help. A teen could hide their sadness from parents who think only adults get depressed. Or a college student might feel guilty for not being able to simply "snap out of it."

These myths can also cause delay in getting needed care. If you believe depression is fake, you might not seek a therapist. If you believe you can fix everything with willpower, you might pass on medication or counseling. The longer you wait, the deeper you might fall into negative thoughts. Myths can rob you of the chance to feel better sooner.

Replacing Myths With Facts

The best way to fight false ideas is with knowledge. When you learn the truth about depression, you can see it for what it is: a valid condition that affects millions of people. You also understand that help is available in many forms. Here are some ways to seek correct information:

1. **Read Trusted Sources**: Look for books or articles by mental health experts. Be sure the information comes from qualified professionals, such as psychologists or psychiatrists.
2. **Talk to Experts**: Counselors and mental health workers can answer questions and clear up confusion. They have studied depression and treated people with many different symptoms.
3. **Join Support Groups**: If possible, you can find in-person or online groups where people discuss depression. Hearing the real stories of others can help you see the truth about this condition.
4. **Listen With an Open Mind**: If a friend or family member has depression, ask them about their experience. Listen carefully to how they feel. This first-hand account can break false beliefs.

Creating a Supportive Environment

We all can help reduce the spread of myths by speaking kindly and factually about depression. Here are simple ways to create a helpful environment:

- **Use Gentle Language**: Avoid saying things like "cheer up." Instead, say, "I'm here to listen" or "How can I help?"
- **Share Facts**: If someone repeats a myth, gently correct them with what you have learned. You can say, "Actually, depression can happen without a big event" or "Kids can have depression, too."
- **Encourage Professional Help**: Suggest seeing a counselor or doctor if someone is showing signs of depression. Remind them it is an act of self-care.

- **Stay Informed**: As new research on depression comes out, keep yourself updated. This helps you stay aware of the best ways to approach and handle depression.

How to Respond When You Hear a Myth

You might hear harmful myths from friends, family, or even people at school. You might feel uncomfortable challenging them, especially if they are grown-ups or authority figures. But you can still respond in a calm and respectful way. If someone says, "Just tough it out," you can reply, "It might feel that way, but depression can need more than just toughness." If they say, "That's not a real thing," you can say, "Many doctors and scientists recognize depression as a real condition."

By sharing small pieces of correct information, you can help change the way people think. Even if they do not believe you right away, you have planted a seed of truth in their mind.

Letting Go of Blame and Shame

Myths often make people blame themselves for being sad. You might think you are not trying hard enough, or that there is something wrong with you. You might feel ashamed to admit you need help. It is very important to let go of this blame and shame. Depression is not your fault. It can happen for many reasons. Even if you made mistakes in the past, that does not mean you caused your depression. Anyone can have it, regardless of their background or life choices.

When you let go of shame, you open the door to seeking real solutions. You can focus on methods to feel better instead of hiding your problems. This can be a huge relief. You might find that your friends and family are more understanding than you thought.

Encouraging Others to Seek Facts

If you have learned the truth about depression, you can share it with those who trust you. If a friend seems to have incorrect ideas, try to correct them gently. If a family member uses hurtful phrases, explain why they might be unhelpful. Encourage them to look at resources from mental health organizations. Sometimes, all it takes is one conversation to start changing false beliefs.

Living Beyond the Myths

Overcoming false ideas is part of taking care of your mental health. When you know the facts, you can recognize your own experiences more clearly. You can spot symptoms that match depression and decide to get help. You can understand that you are not weak or making it up. You can also forgive yourself for not being able to just "snap out of it." This understanding can bring a sense of relief.

Breaking free from myths also lets you see others with more compassion. You realize depression has many faces. It is not limited to a certain age group. It is not always caused by big life events. This insight might help you be kinder and more patient with people who are struggling.

Steps Forward

Here are steps you can take to move forward from this chapter:

1. **Notice Your Thoughts**: Pay attention to any false beliefs you might have held about depression. Replace them with the truths you have learned.
2. **Share Knowledge**: If you see someone repeating a myth, speak up calmly. Offer correct information. You might help someone who is depressed but afraid to admit it.
3. **Question What You Hear**: When someone talks about depression, ask yourself if what they are saying is based on research or just rumors. Stay curious and open to learning more facts.
4. **Talk with Trusted People**: If you think you or a friend could be dealing with depression, talk to a parent, teacher, or counselor. Correct information is the best tool to get the right help.

A Place of Understanding

By exposing these myths, we clear a path to real solutions. People who feel low might see that they are not alone or at fault. They might be more open to talking about their sadness. They might be willing to see a counselor or try other methods. Shifting these beliefs is not just about proving someone wrong. It is about giving you and those around you a fair chance to feel better.

In the next chapters, we will look at more details on signs of depression, healthy ways to handle day-to-day life, and methods that can help you feel more stable. We will also discuss relationships, routines, and activities that can bring moments of relief. Each chapter will give new insights, so you can find tools that work for your situation. Remember that knowledge is power. When you replace myths with facts, you take an important step toward well-being.

Chapter 3: Noting Common Signs

When people think about depression, they often picture someone who feels sad all the time. While sadness is a common part of depression, there are many other signs. These signs can show up in a person's thoughts, emotions, body, and actions. It is helpful to recognize them so that you can know when you or someone you care about might need help. This chapter looks at the signs in more detail and talks about how they might appear in daily life. We will also discuss why it is good to pay attention to changes in habits or mood, even if they seem small.

Emotional Clues

1. **Lingering Sadness**
   One of the main signs of depression is a sadness that does not go away. It might feel like a dull ache that is always there, rather than a sudden burst of tears. You might notice that this sadness gets heavier in the evenings or mornings, or it could stay steady throughout the day. Even if something nice happens, a person with depression may feel little or no lift in mood.
2. **Loss of Joy**
   Depression can make regular activities seem bland or empty. Things that once brought pleasure—like listening to music or talking with friends—might not spark interest anymore. A person could feel numb. They might sit through a favorite movie but feel no excitement or comfort. This change can be subtle at first, but over time, it can become more noticeable.
3. **Feeling Irritable**
   While sadness is expected, some might show anger or crankiness. Feeling on edge can be a sign that a person is struggling inside. Small issues can trigger frustration. A

person might snap at loved ones without knowing why. When the mind is under a lot of stress, it can come out as anger rather than tears.
4. **Hopeless Thoughts**
Depression can bring thoughts that life has no point or that problems cannot be fixed. This might lead to a sense of emptiness. Some describe it as feeling like they are walking through fog, unable to see any reason for hope. They might believe they will never feel better. This can be very hard because it blocks out the idea of seeking help.
5. **Intense Guilt or Shame**
Some people with depression feel guilty about things they did—or did not do—in the past. They might blame themselves for events that were never their fault. This guilt can become overwhelming, feeding negative thoughts and making it hard to feel any sense of peace.

Changes in Thinking

1. **Negative Self-Talk**
People with depression often have negative thoughts about themselves. They might think they are not smart enough or not worthy of love. These thoughts can run in a loop, which makes it tough to break free. Over time, this pattern can worsen symptoms and cause self-doubt.
2. **Trouble Concentrating**
A mind weighed down by depression can have trouble focusing. Homework, reading, or even conversations can become challenging. A person might forget details they just heard. It could feel like the mind is stuck in mud. Tasks that used to be easy take a long time to finish.
3. **Memory Gaps**
Stress and sadness can affect short-term memory. A person might walk into a room and forget why they went there. They

might have trouble recalling what they ate for breakfast. These lapses can lead to more stress, as they realize they are not functioning as smoothly as before.

4. **Indecision**
   Deciding what to wear, what to eat, or what activity to do can feel hard when a person is down. Depression can cause overthinking and fear of making the wrong choice. This might lead to putting off tasks because they feel overwhelming. Even simple decisions can be draining.

5. **Looping Thoughts**
   Some people with depression get stuck in repeating thoughts. They might replay a negative event from the past or worry about the future. This loop can bring anxiety. It can keep the mind busy in an unhelpful way. It can also make it difficult to relax or enjoy the present moment.

Physical Clues

1. **Changes in Sleep**
   One clear sign of depression is an altered sleep schedule. Some people sleep too little and struggle with insomnia. Others find it very hard to get out of bed and end up sleeping for many more hours than usual. Even after sleeping, they may still feel tired.

2. **Appetite Shifts**
   A person with depression might lose interest in food. They may forget to eat or not feel hungry. Some go the other way, eating much more than usual. They might crave comfort foods, like sweets or fried items, in hopes of feeling better. But even eating more does not always relieve the sadness.

3. **Low Energy**
   Depression can make the body feel heavy and sluggish. Everyday tasks, like brushing teeth or preparing breakfast, might seem large and difficult. A person might want to stay in

bed all day because they do not have the energy to face normal tasks.
4. **Physical Pain or Discomfort**
Headaches, muscle aches, or stomach issues can show up in someone with depression. Stress can cause tension in the body, leading to pain. Some people describe a tight feeling in their chest. Others might feel sick in their stomach. These physical problems can be confusing. They may not connect them to depression at first.
5. **Slowed Movement or Speech**
A person might move or talk more slowly than usual. It is not always obvious, but family members might notice a difference. This can be tied to the low energy that comes with depression. It can also be related to sadness weighing on the mind and body.

Changes in Behavior

1. **Avoiding People**
A person with depression may start avoiding social events or gatherings. They might say they are too tired or busy when, in fact, they simply feel unable to interact. They could ignore phone calls or messages because they do not have the energy or desire to respond. This isolation can happen even with close friends.
2. **Loss of Motivation**
Work, school assignments, or chores can feel like climbing a mountain. When motivation drops, deadlines might be missed. Grades can slip. Items around the house might stay undone. The person might appear lazy to others, but inside they could be struggling with deep sadness.
3. **Reckless Actions**
Some cope with their low mood by taking part in risky behaviors. This might mean driving too fast, experimenting

with harmful substances, or picking fights. The person might feel numb and try to feel something—anything—through these actions. They might also feel like they have nothing to lose.

4. **Withdrawing from Favorite Hobbies**
Activities once loved can be abandoned. People with depression might quit sports, music, or art classes. They lose the spark that kept them interested. This withdrawal can make them feel even more alone or bored, contributing to the cycle of sadness.

5. **Trying to Hide Emotions**
People sometimes try to hide what is going on. They might force a smile in front of others. They could act cheerful in social media posts. In private, though, they might feel empty or cry often. This can lead others to think the person is fine, making it harder to spot the signs early on.

Signs in Different Age Groups

1. **Children**
Younger kids might not always be able to say, "I'm depressed." Instead, they could show it through irritability or outbursts. They might have a sudden drop in school performance. They might cling to parents or caregivers more. Some children complain of physical pains like tummy aches when they feel upset. It is important for adults to watch for patterns in behavior.

2. **Teenagers**
Teens can become more withdrawn. They might refuse to talk about their day. Grades can change, or friendships might shift. They could stay up all night and sleep all day. They might show signs of anger or become easily upset. Since teenage years can be filled with new emotions, some people

write off these signs as normal teen behavior. However, it is worth looking closer if the changes become severe.
3. **Adults**
In adults, signs can include missing work, drinking too much, or staying away from family gatherings. Some feel guilty for not being able to meet responsibilities. They might argue more with a partner or friend. Stress about money, jobs, or other problems can make depression worse. Adults may avoid the issue for fear of appearing weak.

Why We Might Overlook the Signs

1. **Stigma**
There is a lingering idea that being sad or down is a sign of weakness. This can lead people to hide their feelings or dismiss them. They may not want to be labeled as someone with depression, so they pretend to be fine.
2. **Lack of Knowledge**
Not everyone learns about mental health. If someone is not taught the signs of depression, they may not recognize what is happening. They might simply think they are "in a bad mood" that will pass. Meanwhile, the symptoms could be getting stronger.
3. **Confusing Signs**
Some symptoms of depression can look like other issues. For example, constant fatigue can also come from a lack of sleep due to a busy schedule. A drop in work performance could be blamed on laziness. People might overlook the deeper cause.
4. **Trying to Stay Positive**
Some folks believe focusing on problems makes them worse. They think ignoring sadness will make it go away. While a positive outlook can help, it does not make a serious condition vanish. It might also lead a person to avoid getting real support.

5. **Fear of Judgement**
   A person might notice changes in themselves but worry that admitting it will lead to gossip. They might fear that friends or family will treat them differently. This fear can be especially strong among teens who worry about fitting in at school.

When to Be Concerned

It can be hard to decide when normal ups and downs become a pattern of depression. Here are some points to watch for:

- **Duration**: If sadness, guilt, or hopelessness last for more than two weeks and do not seem to improve, it might be depression.
- **Impact on Daily Life**: When tasks like bathing, cooking, or studying become too hard, it is a sign that something deeper is going on.
- **Increased Isolation**: If someone stays away from friends or drops out of activities, that can indicate serious inner trouble.
- **Dangerous Thoughts**: Any thoughts about self-harm or feeling like life is not worth living require urgent attention. It is important to reach out right away if you or someone else is having such thoughts.

How to Spot Changes in Yourself

1. **Keep Track**
   Sometimes, writing in a simple diary can help you see changes in your mood or habits. You might notice you are

sleeping too little or too much. You might see patterns in your appetite or energy levels.

2. **Ask for Input**
People close to you might notice changes before you do. If a friend or family member says they are worried, consider their words. It might be hard to hear, but they could be seeing signs that you have overlooked.

3. **Listen to Your Body**
Depression can speak through headaches or stomach aches. If you have frequent pains that do not seem to have a physical cause, it might be worth looking into mental health support. Your body and mind are connected.

4. **Check Your Mood with a Professional**
You can ask for a mental health screening from a doctor or counselor. They can help you see if what you feel lines up with signs of depression. It might feel scary, but getting clarity is a helpful step.

How to Spot Changes in Others

1. **Observe Shifts**
If a friend who used to be lively stops responding to texts or always cancels plans, this might signal a deeper issue. Notice if they look tired or disconnected.

2. **Ask Carefully**
If you suspect a loved one is feeling low, gently ask how they are doing. You could say, "I've noticed you seem tired or a bit down lately. Is everything okay?" This simple question can give them a chance to share if they wish.

3. **Avoid Blame**
Try not to say things like, "Why are you acting like this?" or, "You used to be more fun." This can push them away. Instead, show that you care and are available to listen without judgment.

4. **Encourage Them to Seek Help**
   If they admit they feel hopeless, suggest seeing a counselor or doctor. Offer to help them find resources or go with them if they feel nervous. Let them know they are not alone.

Why Early Awareness Matters

Catching the signs early can mean starting treatment or support sooner. It might prevent the depression from growing worse. Even small steps, like improving sleep or talking with a counselor, can make a difference. If you see a problem in yourself or someone else, do not wait for it to magically go away. Taking action can ease the path toward feeling better.

Steps to Take After Spotting Signs

1. **Talk to Someone Trustworthy**
   This could be a parent, teacher, friend, or counselor. If you are an adult, it might be a coworker, spouse, or mental health professional. Let them know what you have noticed.
2. **Schedule a Check-Up**
   Start with a physical check-up to rule out other health issues. Sometimes, problems with hormones or vitamins can look like depression.
3. **Speak with a Mental Health Expert**
   They can help you figure out if you are dealing with depression or something else. They will talk with you about your feelings and experiences. This is a chance to ask questions and explore possible treatment methods.
4. **Look at Your Routines**
   Though not a total fix, setting a regular bedtime or planning

short walks outside can be an early step. Notice if these small changes provide any relief.
5. **Stay Open-Minded**
   If you have been feeling very low, it is easy to believe nothing can help. Try to remain open to the idea that there are options. Medication, counseling, or support groups can make a difference for many people.

Removing Shame from the Equation

It is important to remember that noticing signs of depression in yourself does not mean something is wrong with you as a person. Having depression is not shameful. It does not mean you are weak. It means you are human. The same goes for noticing signs in others. Showing kindness and support can help people feel less alone. Remember, the earlier you catch these signs, the more quickly you can begin to find relief.

Taking Action

If any of these signs sound familiar, do not ignore them. Acknowledging how you feel is a brave act. It allows you to consider ways to get better. If you know someone else who might be depressed, a thoughtful conversation can be the gentle push they need to look for help. Depression can be harmful when it goes unnoticed, so shining a light on it is vital.

This does not mean you have to fix everything in a day. Depression often needs gradual steps to improve. That is why noting common signs is so valuable. You are doing more than just labeling a problem—you are opening the door to practical changes, whether that means better sleep routines, healthier eating patterns, or professional counseling. Even these small shifts can lead to feeling a bit lighter over time.

Chapter 4: Building Helpful Relationships

Support from other people can be a key factor in feeling better when dealing with depression. Building helpful connections does not mean you have to be best friends with everyone you meet. It also does not mean your relationships must be perfect. Instead, it means finding and growing bonds with people who offer understanding, respect, and compassion. This chapter will explore ways to create and maintain those connections in different parts of your life, such as at home, at school or work, and in the community.

The Power of Human Connection

Human beings are social by nature, even if some people prefer more time alone than others. We often feel safer and more at ease when we have at least one person who cares about us. For a person with depression, isolation can make sadness worse. Spending too much time alone can allow negative thoughts to grow. Having someone to talk with, laugh with, or just sit quietly with can help ease stress.

When you share your thoughts with a trusted person, you create a space for understanding. That person can provide emotional support and help you feel less alone. Even if they cannot solve your problems, the simple act of listening is often valuable. Having a caring ear can remind you that your feelings matter.

Types of Supportive Connections

1. **Family**
   Family members can be strong pillars of support, though not every family is warm and open. If you have caring family members, you may find comfort in telling them how you feel.

A parent, sibling, or other close relative might help you find a counselor or manage daily tasks when you are feeling low.

2. **Friends**

    Friends can sometimes relate to your experiences, especially if they are around your age. They might also have gone through sadness or know someone who has. True friends do not judge or make fun of you for being vulnerable. They offer encouragement when you need it and respect your feelings.

3. **Teachers or Mentors**

    At school, a teacher might notice if you are behaving differently or not keeping up. If you trust them, you can talk to them privately. They may help you get in touch with a school counselor or adjust your workload if stress at school is contributing to your low mood.

4. **Coworkers or Supervisors**

    In the workplace, you could have a coworker who you trust enough to share brief updates about how you feel. While it may not be appropriate to share in detail during working hours, letting a supervisor know you are struggling can sometimes lead to adjustments. You might be given more flexible deadlines or be allowed to work from home if that is possible.

5. **Neighbors and Community Members**

    People in your neighborhood or local community centers can also be supportive. They might lead local clubs or activities. Just having someone to say hello to can help you feel part of a group. Community events like small gatherings or charitable activities can be ways to connect with others.

6. **Support Groups**

    These are groups that meet specifically to talk about mental health. People share stories of their struggles and victories. These groups often operate online too. Support groups can make you realize you are not the only person facing these feelings.

Qualities of a Helpful Relationship

Not all relationships are equal. Some can be unhealthy, making you feel judged or ignored. Others can be safe and supportive, which you need when facing depression. Here are some qualities to look for:

1. **Listening Skills**
   You want someone who truly listens, rather than waiting to give their own opinions right away. They should give you space to speak and clarify if they do not understand something.
2. **Kindness**
   A helper shows kindness by offering gentle words and actions. They do not shame you for having a hard time. They do not force you to be cheerful on command. Instead, they give empathy.
3. **Respect**
   Respect involves honoring your boundaries and privacy. A respectful person does not share your personal stories with others without your permission. They also avoid pushing you into choices that you are not ready to make.
4. **Trustworthiness**
   You should feel safe opening up. If a friend or family member has betrayed your trust in the past, you might be hesitant. Find someone who proves by their actions that they will be reliable. Over time, you can share more with them.
5. **Consistency**
   It is normal for people to be busy sometimes, but a helpful relationship has some level of regular contact. It might be a quick call once a week or a text every few days. Having someone who checks in can help you feel grounded.

Building New Connections

You might feel like you do not have anyone to turn to. In that case, building new connections is possible, though it can take time. Here are some ways to start:

1. **Try Simple Greetings**
   Whether at school, work, or in your neighborhood, practice a friendly greeting. You do not have to jump into deep conversation right away. Over time, these small interactions can build comfort.
2. **Join a Local Group**
   If you like reading, see if there is a library group. If you enjoy gardening, find a neighborhood project. Any shared interest can be a starting point for conversation. You might find people who share your hobby and are also open to making new friends.
3. **Use Online Communities Wisely**
   There are many online forums where people discuss mental health or particular interests. Look for forums that are known to be caring and moderated. Be careful not to share personal details like your address or phone number right away. Online connections can lead to friendships, but stay safe.
4. **Attend Community Events**
   Open houses, local fairs, or volunteer drives are good places to meet people with similar passions. If you are shy, going with a friend or family member might help. Remember, you do not have to make a best friend on day one. Just being around others can be a step toward feeling less alone.

Communicating Your Needs

1. **Be Honest About Your Feelings**
   If you decide to share with someone you trust, say something

like, "I've been feeling really low lately, and it is affecting my daily life." This gives them a clear picture. They might ask how they can help, or they might just listen.

2. **Say What You Need**
People cannot read your mind. If you need someone to spend a bit more time with you, let them know. If you just want a listening ear rather than advice, say so. Setting these guidelines can help avoid misunderstandings.

3. **Stay Open to Their Response**
The person might have questions or might not know what to say right away. That is okay. Talking about mental health can be new for them too. Be patient as they figure out how to respond.

4. **Respect Boundaries**
While you are sharing, remember the other person also has limits. They may not be available all the time. They might also feel unsure about how to help. Encourage them to speak up if they feel overwhelmed, and be willing to seek professional help if you need more than they can offer.

Handling Reactions

When you share that you are feeling depressed, you might get different reactions:

1. **Support and Understanding**
Some people will appreciate that you trusted them. They may offer a shoulder to lean on or help you explore solutions. This is the best-case scenario.

2. **Confusion or Lack of Knowledge**
Not everyone understands depression. They might say things like, "But you look fine," or "Just cheer up." This does not mean they do not care. They might just not know how to

handle the topic. Gently explaining that depression is more than just sadness can help.

3. **Dismissal**
Unfortunately, some people might not take you seriously. They might even make fun of you or accuse you of seeking attention. If this happens, it is important to turn to others who are kinder. Do not blame yourself for their reaction.

4. **Fear**
Sometimes, people worry they will say the wrong thing. They might pull back. If someone is afraid to talk about mental health, you can suggest they read reliable sources or speak with a counselor themselves to learn how to support you better.

Strengthening Existing Bonds

If you already have friends or relatives you care about, you can strengthen these ties:

1. **Regular Check-Ins**
Agree to a set time to catch up, whether by phone, video call, or in person. This keeps communication open and makes it easier for you to share updates on your mood.

2. **Shared Activities**
Doing things together can boost your spirits. You could go for a walk, cook a simple meal, or watch a favorite show. Spending quality time can also remind you that you have support.

3. **Honest Conversations**
Let your loved ones know if something they do is unhelpful. For example, if they keep telling you to "get over it," explain why that hurts. Healthy relationships can handle honest feedback. If the person cares, they will try to adjust.

4. **Offer Support in Return**
   Relationships are a two-way street. Even though you might be feeling low, try to also be there for them when they have concerns. This balance can help you avoid feeling like a burden.

Dealing with Unhelpful Relationships

In some cases, relationships can hurt more than help:

1. **Toxic Friendships**
   A toxic friend might insult you or only call you when they need something. They may dismiss your problems but expect you to solve theirs. If you constantly feel worse after speaking with them, it might be time to reduce contact.
2. **Abusive Family Members**
   If a family member is abusive—physically, emotionally, or verbally—you should seek help from a teacher, counselor, or trusted friend. No one should face abuse, and it can worsen depression.
3. **Unhealthy Romantic Partners**
   A partner who does not respect your feelings or tries to control you is not healthy for your mental well-being. It might be hard to end such a relationship, but staying can cause more harm. Consider reaching out to a counselor for guidance.
4. **Conflicts That Are Not Resolved**
   Arguments or disagreements can occur in any relationship. But if they constantly remain unresolved, they can add to your stress. Trying to calmly address problems or seeking the help of a mediator (such as a counselor) can sometimes fix the conflict. If it cannot be fixed, you may need some distance for your own well-being.

Finding Professional Support

1. **Therapists and Counselors**
   These professionals are trained to help people with mental health concerns. They can guide you in learning coping tools. They can also help you work through negative thoughts or old hurts that fuel your depression.
2. **Psychiatrists**
   These are medical doctors who can discuss if medication might help. Medication is not a cure by itself, but it can relieve some symptoms. A psychiatrist can work together with a counselor so you receive a complete approach.
3. **Group Therapy**
   Group therapy sessions give you a chance to hear from others facing similar feelings. A therapist leads the group, helping members share experiences and practice social skills. This can reduce feelings of isolation.
4. **Crisis Hotlines**
   If you are feeling extremely low and need immediate help, crisis hotlines offer round-the-clock support. Trained volunteers or counselors will listen and guide you toward further help.

Supporting Someone Who Is Depressed

If you are trying to support a friend or family member:

1. **Listen More Than You Talk**
   Let the person express their feelings without cutting them off. Ask clarifying questions if needed. Just being there can mean a lot.
2. **Encourage Positive Steps**
   Without forcing them, gently suggest they try small changes like a short walk or a visit to the doctor. Offer to go with them if it helps.

3. **Avoid Shaming**
   Do not say things like, "Others have it worse," or "You should be grateful." These statements can make them feel invalidated. It is more helpful to say, "I'm sorry you're feeling this way. How can I help?"
4. **Set Your Own Limits**
   Supporting someone can be tough. Make sure you also look after your well-being. If you feel overwhelmed, it is okay to suggest they speak to a counselor for extra help.

Balancing Online and Offline Relationships

In modern times, some people have strong online friendships. While these can be valuable, it is also important to have some real-world interactions if possible. Offline interactions allow you to sense body language, facial expressions, and tone of voice. Online friends might not notice if you skip meals or look tired. On the other hand, online communities can be a great source of support, especially if local support is limited.

It can be best to have a mix of both. Keep in touch with online friends who understand your struggles, but also try to build real-life connections. This balance can make you feel more secure overall.

Small Steps Make a Difference

It might feel like a big leap to talk about depression or to open up about deep feelings. But remember that relationships grow over time. You can start with small talks about general topics, then share more when you feel ready. Every time you connect with someone who cares, you are adding a piece of support to your life. Even if they cannot solve your problems, just having someone who will listen can ease the weight on your mind.

Chapter 5: Using Healthy Routines

When dealing with deep sadness or low mood, it can seem like every day blends together. You might struggle to find purpose in small tasks. You might wake up late, forget to do important chores, and feel tired or lost. This is where a stable routine can help. A routine is a pattern of actions you do at certain times or in a certain order. It is like a map that guides you through each day.

This chapter will discuss the benefits of having healthy routines, how to form a routine that fits your life, and how to adjust it if you find it is not working for you. We will also look at small ideas you can add to your day that can support better mood management. By trying out these ideas, you can provide yourself with structure, which can help you feel more steady during hard times.

Why Routines Matter

1. **A Sense of Control**
   When sadness or anxiety takes over, it can feel like your life is spinning. Having a routine, even if it is simple, gives you a sense of control. You decide when to wake up, when to have meals, and when to spend time relaxing. This can help you remember that some things are still in your hands.
2. **Reduced Stress**
   Uncertainty can add to stress. If you do not know what to do next, you can feel uneasy. A schedule removes some of that uncertainty. For example, if you know that every evening you spend 30 minutes tidying up your space, you do not have to wonder when you will get it done. This reduces the mental load of making decisions under stress.
3. **Better Sleep and Meals**
   Going to bed and waking up around the same time can help regulate your body's internal clock. Eating at regular times

can support stable energy levels. Over time, these habits can support both physical and mental health, making your mood less likely to swing sharply.
4. **Steady Progress**
Depression can make even small tasks feel huge. A routine breaks the day into smaller steps. It can help you do tasks bit by bit. By completing small items on your schedule, you experience small moments of success that can counter feelings of worthlessness.
5. **Fewer Last-Minute Surprises**
Planning ahead can prevent a buildup of tasks that must be done all at once. For instance, if you always do a bit of laundry on Wednesday, you do not reach the weekend buried in clothes. Preventing these last-minute rushes can keep tension down.

Choosing a Simple Start

Not everyone can jump into a full day's schedule overnight. Begin with small, easy changes. For instance, pick one or two tasks you plan to do at about the same time daily. Examples might be:

- **Waking up at 7 a.m.** on weekdays
- **Having breakfast by 8 a.m.** each day
- **Taking a short walk in the late afternoon**

These are just examples. The point is to pick small targets that are realistic for your life. If you already wake up at 9 a.m., do not try to force yourself to wake up at 5 a.m. right away. That can be too big a shift and can lead to failure and added frustration.

Mapping Out Your Day

1. **Morning Routine**
    - **Wake-Up Time**: Choose a time that gives you enough rest but also does not allow you to stay in bed all day.

- **Morning Activity**: A short moment to stretch, read something calm, or do light breathing can set a positive tone. You can even do something as simple as drinking a glass of water while taking a few slow breaths.
- **Personal Hygiene**: Try to shower or wash your face. Changing out of your sleepwear, even if you are not leaving the house, can shift your mindset from sleep to wakefulness.

2. **Midday Routine**
    - **Meal Times**: Having lunch around the same time daily helps keep energy levels more steady.
    - **A Planned Break**: If you have school or work, schedule a 10- to 15-minute break. Use that time to step outside or close your eyes and breathe slowly.
    - **Work or Study Block**: If you have tasks to complete, dedicate a set window of time for them. This helps you focus better, knowing you have set aside that period for tasks.

3. **Afternoon or Evening Routine**
    - **Homework or Chores**: It might help to do chores at the same time daily, so they do not pile up.
    - **Physical Movement**: This does not have to be high-intensity exercise (we will talk more about exercise in a later chapter). Even a short walk or some gentle stretching can help clear your mind.
    - **Relaxing Activity**: Plan something calming toward the late afternoon or early evening. It could be reading a fun book, listening to soothing music, or playing a quiet game.

4. **Night Routine**
    - **Winding Down**: About an hour before bed, try to reduce bright lights and loud sounds. Set aside electronic devices if possible. This helps your brain know that bedtime is coming.

- **Calming Habit**: Some people like to journal or read a few pages of a book. Others might do gentle stretches. This can help you enter a relaxed state.
- **Bedtime**: Choose a target bedtime that allows for enough sleep. If you struggle to fall asleep, keep the same bedtime anyway. Over time, your body might adjust.

Handling Distractions and Setbacks

Even with a plan, life can get in the way. You might oversleep or get stuck doing something else. You might feel too low to follow the plan. Try these ideas:

1. **Give Yourself Slack**
   If you miss a task, try not to be too hard on yourself. You can aim to do better the next day. A routine is meant to guide you, not make you feel worse.
2. **Use Reminders**
   Alarms on your phone, a paper planner, or sticky notes can prompt you to do tasks at certain times. This is helpful if you have trouble focusing or if you get distracted easily.
3. **Limit Screen Time During Important Tasks**
   Phones and computers can draw you in. Consider putting them on silent or placing them out of reach when you want to complete a task. This can help you stay on track.
4. **Adjust When Needed**
   If a certain time slot keeps failing (for example, you keep missing a 6 a.m. walk because you are not a morning person), change the schedule. Move the walk to midday or after work. It is better to adjust than to give up on the idea of a walk altogether.

Adding Positive Moments to Your Routine

Part of managing depression is creating small pockets of relief or moments that make you feel calmer. Here are a few ways to weave these into your schedule:

1. **Plan Short Joyful Activities**
   Even if you do not feel a rush of happiness, doing something that used to please you can be helpful in small doses. It could be 10 minutes of doodling or listening to an uplifting tune. Over time, these small slices of enjoyment might remind you that life has pleasant aspects too.
2. **Check in With a Friend**
   If you have a supportive friend, schedule a chat at least once a week. It could be a quick phone call or a video call. Talking to someone who cares can help break isolation.
3. **Include Gratitude Exercises**
   While you might not feel grateful for big things when you are depressed, you can take note of small comforts. For example, if the weather was nice or you had a tasty meal, jot it down. Doing this regularly can shift your mind toward noticing things that are okay or helpful in your life.
4. **Deep Breathing Times**
   Make it a habit to pause once or twice a day to take slow, deep breaths for a minute or two. This can help calm racing thoughts or tension in the body.

Balancing Work or School With Self-Care

1. **Set Clear Boundaries**
   Whether you are a student or have a job, try to decide on certain hours for working and certain hours for resting. This helps prevent burnout, which can worsen depression.

2. **Break Tasks Down**
   If a school project or a work duty feels huge, split it into smaller tasks. Plan to finish one part each day. This way, the job is more manageable.
3. **Use Tools to Stay Organized**
   A calendar or a to-do list app can help you see what must be done and when. Cross off tasks as you complete them. This simple action can bring a small sense of satisfaction.
4. **Communicate Needs**
   If possible, let teachers, employers, or teammates know when you are overwhelmed. This might feel awkward, but they cannot support you if they do not know what you are facing. They might offer more time or help delegate tasks to someone else.

The Role of Flexibility

A routine should help you, not trap you. Depression can vary from day to day. Some days, you may have the energy to follow your plan. Other days, getting out of bed can be a challenge. Allow yourself room to shift things around:

- **Skip a Task if Truly Needed**: If you feel physically unwell or extremely low, it might be okay to skip one non-urgent task. The key is to resume your routine the next day or when you feel capable.
- **Rotate Activities**: If taking an evening walk becomes boring or too difficult, switch to gentle stretching at home. It still provides some movement but may be easier on days when you feel slow.
- **Plan for Emergencies**: Life can throw you a curveball. If you have an exam or a last-minute family event, your schedule might shift. Prepare a "Plan B" for these moments. Maybe you

will do a shorter version of your tasks or postpone them with the intention to return soon.

Using Routines to Track Changes

Your routine can also act as a tool for noticing changes in your mood or energy. If you track how you feel each day (even with simple notes like "felt very tired" or "felt okay"), you might spot patterns. For example:

- **Days of Low Mood After Poor Sleep**: You might see that on nights when you only got 4 hours of sleep, you felt much worse the next day.
- **Improvement After a Certain Activity**: You may find that on days when you took a 15-minute morning walk, you felt a bit more alert later.
- **Changes During Stressful Times**: If there is a busy period at school or a problem at work, you can see how it affects your ability to stick to the routine.

These notes can help you figure out what works best for you. They can also provide information to share with a counselor or doctor if you decide to seek professional support.

Ideas for Different Lifestyles

1. **For Students**
    - **Create a Homework Block**: Dedicate a set hour or two after school for homework. Then give yourself a planned rest before bedtime.
    - **Study Groups**: If you feel alone, see if you can study with a friend once or twice a week. It mixes social time with getting things done.

2. **For Working Adults**
    - **Daily Check of Tasks**: First thing in the morning, review your main goals for the workday. Make sure they are realistic.
    - **Regular Breaks**: Taking a 5-minute break every hour or two can keep your mind from getting too overwhelmed. Use that time to stretch or sip water.
3. **For Those At Home**
    - **Organize Household Tasks**: Map out tasks like laundry, cooking, or cleaning on different days. This spreads out the chores so you do not face them all at once.
    - **Scheduled Social Interactions**: If you spend most of your time at home, plan calls or visits to avoid feeling isolated.

Staying Motivated

Motivation can be hard to come by when you are depressed. But routines can provide some momentum even when motivation is low. The idea is that you do not need to feel motivated to do the task if it is scheduled into your day. You follow the plan because it is time to do it. Over time, completing tasks can lead to a small sense of accomplishment, which can help lift your mood bit by bit.

It also helps to reward yourself in simple ways. For instance, if you manage to stick to your routine for a week, you might allow yourself an hour of a special activity you find soothing (like reading a lighthearted book or watching a calming show). These small rewards can keep you engaged with the routine.

Avoiding Perfectionism

Having a routine does not mean everything must be perfect. Perfectionism can create pressure, which can worsen stress. Here are a few tips to avoid that trap:

1. **Accept Partial Success**
   If you planned to do 30 minutes of cleaning but only did 15, that is still progress. Acknowledge that you tried.
2. **Be Kind to Yourself**
   Treat yourself like you would treat a friend. If you would reassure a friend that it is okay not to meet every goal, do the same for yourself.
3. **Adjust Goals**
   If you find you are missing a goal often, it may be too big or at the wrong time. Reduce the difficulty or change the time slot. A workable routine is better than a perfect but impossible one.

Combining Routine With Other Support

A healthy routine is only one piece of managing depression. It can be combined with:

- **Therapy or Counseling**: A counselor can help you shape a routine that fits your lifestyle and mental health needs.
- **Medication**: If you are on medication, taking it at the same time daily can be part of your schedule.
- **Support Groups**: You might plan your schedule around attending group meetings, which can further help you stay connected.
- **Physical Exercise**: Chapter 7 will address staying active in more detail, but you can put short exercise breaks into your daily plan.

By combining a routine with other methods, you increase the chance of feeling more stable and seeing improvements over time.

Building on Each Success

When you first begin, it might feel strange to follow a schedule if you are not used to it. You might also worry that you will fail. But each time you follow your routine—even in a small way—you are practicing a helpful habit. For example, if you managed to go to bed at your chosen bedtime three nights out of seven, that is a step in the right direction. Next week, aim for four nights. Bit by bit, the routine becomes part of your life.

If you find a routine is truly not helpful or it makes you feel worse, talk to a mental health professional or a trusted friend about why. Sometimes, certain activities in the schedule need to be replaced with tasks you find calmer or more suitable. The main point is to shape a routine that reduces stress rather than adding to it.

Real-Life Example

Here is a brief story to illustrate how a routine can help. Imagine a student named Mariah who feels down most mornings and stays in bed until noon on weekends. She notices that once she finally gets up, half the day is gone, and she feels guilty. She also goes to sleep very late. To change this, she decides on a routine:

- **Wake up at 9 a.m. on Saturday and Sunday.**
- **Spend 15 minutes stretching or writing in a journal.**
- **Eat a simple breakfast (like cereal) by 10 a.m.**

At first, Mariah struggles to get up at 9 a.m. She manages 9:30 a.m. the first weekend. Still, it is earlier than noon, and she tries not to feel bad about the difference. She notices that eating breakfast helps her feel a little more awake. Over a few weeks, she is able to get out of bed closer to 9 a.m. more often. She adds a short walk at 4 p.m. and starts feeling a bit more in control of her day. She is not suddenly free of sadness, but having a plan lessens her sense of helplessness.

Putting It All Together

A healthy routine can act as a frame to hold you up when depression tries to pull you down. It does not have to be strict or full of complicated tasks. Instead, think of it as a friendly guide that points you toward basic self-care steps and small bits of progress each day. If you find yourself too tired or low to follow the plan, be gentle with yourself and try again next time.

Remember:

- **Start small** to avoid feeling overwhelmed.
- **Plan key tasks** (wake-up time, meals, chores) at times that make sense for you.
- **Add brief moments** of rest or calm.
- **Stay flexible** and adjust as needed.
- **Combine your routine** with other support methods like counseling or talking to a trusted person.

Through these steps, you may notice that the days start to have a bit more structure and a bit less chaos. While depression can still be present, it becomes more manageable when you have a plan to guide you. Even if you only follow part of the plan each day, you are setting a foundation to build on. This foundation, over time, can help you move toward a steadier emotional state.

Chapter 6: Eating Well

Many people overlook how much food choices can affect mood. When sadness or worry takes over, you might lose your appetite or eat more than usual. You might grab quick snacks or skip meals. These eating habits can make depression symptoms worse. On the other hand, balanced meals can help your body and mind function better.

This chapter explores why healthy eating matters, how certain foods can support mood, and how to make better food choices even when you feel low. You do not need to become a nutrition expert overnight or follow strict diets. Instead, focus on simple adjustments that can help you feel stronger and more balanced each day.

Why Eating Habits Affect Mood

1. **Energy Levels**
   Food gives you fuel. If you skip meals, your energy might dip, causing fatigue and irritability. Eating regular, balanced meals keeps your energy more steady, which can help you handle daily tasks with less strain.
2. **Blood Sugar Swings**
   Foods high in sugar can cause a quick rise in energy, followed by a crash. This up-and-down pattern can affect mood and attention. Choosing steadier sources of energy—like whole grains—can keep your blood sugar from swinging too wildly.
3. **Nutrients for the Brain**
   Your brain needs certain vitamins and minerals to produce chemicals that regulate mood. For instance, B vitamins and magnesium help support healthy brain function. If your body lacks these nutrients, you could experience increased fatigue or stress.

4. **Connection to Sleep**
   Heavy or spicy meals late at night can interfere with restful sleep. Poor sleep can worsen depression. Also, not eating enough during the day might make you too hungry at bedtime, which can disrupt sleep. Balanced food intake supports better rest.

Common Eating Struggles During Depression

1. **Loss of Appetite**
   You might feel no desire to eat. Food might not taste good, or you may feel too tired to prepare a meal. Over time, not eating enough can lead to weakness and worsen mood swings.
2. **Overeating or Emotional Eating**
   Some people turn to comfort foods to cope with sadness. This might provide a brief sense of relief, but overeating can lead to guilt or physical discomfort. It also may contribute to health problems in the long run.
3. **Skipping Meals**
   Whether it is from lack of appetite or disorganization, skipping meals can become a habit. This can cause your body to run on low fuel, raising stress hormones and making you feel more anxious or down.
4. **Reliance on Processed Foods**
   When you do not feel like cooking, it is easy to grab packaged snacks or fast food. These items often lack key nutrients and have high sugar or salt. While convenient, they might make you feel sluggish or moody later.

Building Better Eating Patterns

1. **Start with Small Changes**
   Big changes to your diet can be overwhelming when you are already dealing with depression. Choose one or two goals to work on first. Examples:
   - Drink an extra glass of water daily.
   - Eat breakfast at least three times a week if you usually skip it.
2. **Plan Simple Meals**
   You do not need fancy recipes. A balanced plate could include:
   - A source of protein (chicken, beans, tofu, eggs).
   - A source of complex carbohydrates (brown rice, whole wheat bread, oats).
   - A vegetable or fruit (fresh, frozen, or canned in natural juice).
3. If you find it hard to prepare full meals, look for easy options like a turkey sandwich on whole grain bread with lettuce and tomato.
4. **Regular Meal Times**
   Try to set approximate times for breakfast, lunch, and dinner. You can adjust these to fit your schedule. The goal is to avoid long gaps without eating. Consistent meal times help keep your energy levels steady.
5. **Balance Food Groups**
   While you do not need to obsess over every nutrient, aim for variety over the course of a week. This could mean having some fruit in the morning, some vegetables at lunch, and a protein like fish or chicken at dinner.

Mindful Eating

1. **Slow Down**
   If you rush through meals, you might not notice what or how much you are eating. Eating slowly allows your body to register fullness and enjoyment. It can also reduce stress because you are giving yourself a quiet break.
2. **Pay Attention to Flavors and Textures**
   Try to notice the taste of your food, the crunch or softness, and the smell. By being present in the moment, you may find a tiny bit of comfort in the process of eating. This also helps shift your thoughts away from negative thinking, if only for a short while.
3. **Watch Emotional Triggers**
   Before reaching for a snack, ask yourself if you are truly hungry or just stressed or sad. If you are not hungry, consider another way to manage that feeling—like taking a short walk or talking to someone.
4. **Avoid Distractions**
   Eating in front of the TV or scrolling on a phone can lead to mindless snacking. If possible, set aside mealtime as device-free to help you stay aware of what you are putting into your body.

Foods That Can Support Mood

While no single food is a magic cure for depression, some items might help support a steadier mindset:

1. **Whole Grains**
   Brown rice, whole wheat bread, oatmeal, and quinoa provide fiber and steady energy. This helps avoid sudden crashes in blood sugar that can affect mood.

2. **Lean Proteins**
   Chicken, turkey, fish, beans, and lentils are examples of protein sources. Protein is needed for many bodily functions, including the making of mood-related chemicals in the brain.
3. **Fruits and Vegetables**
   They offer vitamins, minerals, and antioxidants that support overall health. Adding different colored produce (like carrots, spinach, berries) can supply a range of helpful nutrients.
4. **Nuts and Seeds**
   Walnuts, almonds, flaxseeds, and chia seeds contain healthy fats. They can also provide magnesium and other nutrients that help with stress management.
5. **Water**
   Staying hydrated is often overlooked but very important. Dehydration can cause tiredness and headaches, which can worsen a low mood.
6. **Dairy or Dairy Alternatives**
   Items like low-fat yogurt or fortified non-dairy milk can offer calcium and vitamin D, which support healthy bones and may aid in mood regulation.

Comfort Foods in Moderation

It is fine to enjoy foods that you find comforting. However, try to keep them balanced with healthier choices. A small treat now and then will not destroy your diet. The problems arise when you rely on sweets, chips, or fried foods as a main part of your eating plan. If you notice you keep reaching for sugary snacks whenever you feel sad, try placing a bowl of fruit or a healthier snack option where it is easy to grab.

Practical Tips for Shopping and Meal Prep

1. **Make a Simple Grocery List**
   Before you head to the store or order groceries, plan a few basic meals for the week. Write down ingredients so you have what you need. This reduces random buys and helps you stick to more balanced choices.
2. **Shop the Outer Sections**
   In many stores, the outer edges have fresh fruits, vegetables, dairy, meats, and whole grains. The inner aisles often hold more processed foods. While you still might visit the inner aisles for items like beans or whole grain pasta, focusing on fresh produce can encourage healthier meals.
3. **Batch Cooking**
   If you have enough energy or help from family or friends, try cooking a large batch of something simple, like soup or chili. Store portions in containers, so you can heat them up for quick lunches or dinners throughout the week. This can be a lifesaver on days when you are too tired to cook from scratch.
4. **Use Frozen or Canned Foods**
   Fresh produce can be expensive or spoil quickly. Frozen vegetables and fruits are usually picked at their best and can be just as nutritious. Canned beans or vegetables (with low salt) are also good for quick and affordable meals.
5. **Cook Together with Others**
   If you live with family or roommates, consider cooking as a shared activity. Not only does it split the work, but you can enjoy a bit of social time. For some, cooking with a friend provides motivation to prepare a proper meal rather than skipping it.

Overcoming Barriers to Healthy Eating

1. **Low Motivation**
   Depression can sap your will to plan and cook meals. If you cannot manage a full cooking session, at least prepare simpler options. A peanut butter and banana sandwich can be a better choice than skipping a meal entirely.
2. **Cost Concerns**
   Healthy eating does not have to be expensive. Look for sales, buy produce in season, and consider store-brand items. Dried beans, rice, and oats are often cheap and can be used in many meals.
3. **Lack of Cooking Skills**
   If you are unsure how to cook, start with basic recipes. There are many free videos and guides online. Simple meals like scrambled eggs, veggie stir-fry, or pasta with tomato sauce require minimal practice.
4. **Cravings for Junk Food**
   Cravings often come from habit or emotional triggers. If you want to reduce cravings, do not stock large amounts of junk food at home. Instead, keep fruit, whole grain crackers, or yogurt on hand. If a craving hits, try drinking water first or waiting 10 minutes to see if the urge passes.

Listening to Your Body

Paying attention to how foods make you feel can guide your choices:

- **Log Your Meals**: For a week, jot down what you eat and how you feel afterward. Notice patterns. Do you get a headache when you skip lunch? Do you feel less anxious after a balanced breakfast?
- **Check for Food Sensitivities**: Some people feel bloated or uncomfortable after eating certain foods. If you suspect a

food makes you feel bad, you might want to talk to a doctor about possible allergies or sensitivities.
- **Variety Over Restriction**: Rather than cutting out entire food groups without medical advice, aim for a broad range of nutrient-dense foods. Too many rules can add stress.

Special Considerations

1. **Medication Interactions**
   If you are on any medication, ask your doctor if there are foods you should avoid. Some medications react with certain items. For instance, certain antidepressants might not go well with high amounts of particular foods or drinks.
2. **Supplements**
   Some people consider supplements like multivitamins or fish oil. It is best to talk to a doctor first. Supplements are not a replacement for real food, but they can fill in gaps if you cannot get all nutrients from your diet alone.
3. **Eating Disorders**
   If you suspect you have a troubled relationship with food—such as obsessive dieting, binging, or purging—share this with a trusted professional. Eating disorders are serious conditions that often need specialized help.

Planning for Snack Attacks

Snacks can be part of a healthy eating plan, especially if you pick options that give nutrients:

- **Fruit with Nut Butter**: Apple slices with peanut butter.
- **Veggies and Hummus**: Carrot sticks or cucumber slices dipped in hummus.

- **Cheese and Crackers**: Choose whole grain crackers for more fiber.
- **Greek Yogurt with Berries**: A protein-rich option that also offers vitamins.
- **Mixed Nuts**: Aim for unsalted or lightly salted if possible.

Keep these kinds of snacks ready to go, so you are less tempted to grab chips or candy. If you still want a sweet treat, limit the portion size. For instance, instead of a whole bar of chocolate, eat a few small squares and savor them slowly.

Eating Socially

1. **Shared Meals**
   If you feel lonely, eating with others can make mealtime more pleasant. Invite a friend for lunch or cook with a roommate.
2. **Potluck Style**
   If you have a group of friends or family, each person can bring one dish. This cuts down on the work for each individual.
3. **Respect Your Comfort Level**
   If large gatherings make you anxious, try smaller meet-ups. The goal is to enjoy shared food without feeling overwhelmed.

Celebrating Small Wins

When you manage to eat more balanced meals or you try new recipes, acknowledge that you did something positive for yourself. Recognizing these steps can help you stay encouraged. For instance, if you made a homemade meal instead of ordering fast food, note that as a good choice. If you found a new fruit or vegetable you like, keep it on your grocery list. These small moments can make you feel more capable.

Combining Eating Well with Other Strategies

Healthy eating on its own might not erase all symptoms of depression, but it can make a useful difference in how you feel each day. Combine it with:

- **A Consistent Routine**: Have set times to eat so you do not forget.
- **Physical Activity**: Light exercise can help regulate appetite and mood.
- **Stress Management**: If you feel overwhelmed, practice simple calming methods.
- **Professional Help**: Doctors and counselors can offer advice that fits your unique needs.

A Realistic Approach

You do not need a flawless diet. Aim for balance over time. If you slip up and skip a meal or eat a bag of chips late at night, that does not ruin everything. Notice the slip, see if there is a reason (like stress or lack of planning), and try to do better for the next meal. A pattern of mostly balanced choices can still help your mind and body function better.

Also, remember that taste buds can change. If you are used to very sugary or salty foods, healthier options might seem bland at first. Give it time. Slowly lower the amount of sugar or salt you use. Add herbs and spices to bring flavor without relying solely on salt. Over several weeks, your preferences might shift.

Example Day of Balanced Eating

Below is a simple example of how you might spread out your meals. Adjust portion sizes and foods based on personal preference or dietary needs:

- **Breakfast**: Oatmeal with berries and a sprinkle of chopped nuts. Drink water or tea.
- **Mid-Morning Snack**: A banana or a small handful of almonds.
- **Lunch**: A sandwich with whole grain bread, lean turkey, lettuce, tomato, and a side of carrots.
- **Afternoon Snack**: Low-fat yogurt with a drizzle of honey.
- **Dinner**: Salmon or chicken (baked or grilled), brown rice, and steamed broccoli.
- **Evening Option**: If you are still hungry or want a light snack, have a piece of fruit or a cup of warm milk.

This plan is just an example. Feel free to swap items based on what you have available or what you like.

Looking Ahead

Eating well is a supportive act you can do for yourself. When depressed, it might feel like one more chore. But healthy meals help you keep your body and mind in better shape, which can ease some strain. Combine this approach with the routines discussed earlier. Plan meals ahead when possible, keep nutritious snacks at hand, and try to avoid long stretches without food.

Chapter 7: Staying Physically Active

A low mood can make it tough to move around and exercise. When you feel sad or exhausted, even the idea of walking to the mailbox can seem too big. But staying active, in whatever way your body can manage, can be a helpful piece of caring for your mind. You do not have to run a marathon or become a skilled athlete. Even gentle movements can bring benefits. This chapter will look at how physical activity can help mood, different ways to move your body, and tips to stay motivated when energy is low.

Why Activity Helps Mood

1. **Chemical Changes in the Brain**
   When you exercise, your body releases chemicals that can improve mood. These include endorphins, which can bring a small sense of relief or calm. They also include other helpful substances that support the parts of the brain linked to feeling stable. Over time, these chemicals can make it easier to manage sadness or worry.
2. **Reduced Stress**
   Moving your body can help clear tense feelings. If you have a lot on your mind, doing an activity like walking or dancing can shift your focus. When you are done, you might notice that some of your worries seem a bit lighter. Your body can also feel more relaxed.
3. **Better Sleep**
   Physical activity during the day can help you feel more ready to sleep at night. Improved sleep often leads to clearer thinking and less moodiness. However, try not to do high-energy exercises too close to bedtime. That can make it harder to wind down.

4. **Confidence Boost**
   Each time you do an activity—whether it is a short stroll or a short workout—you build a sense of ability. Over time, seeing small improvements, like walking a bit farther or doing more steps, can bring a sense of achievement. You might realize you are stronger than you thought.
5. **Healthy Distraction**
   Depression can cause your thoughts to swirl around sad or negative topics. Doing a physical task can break that loop for a while. This healthy distraction might help you avoid dwelling on problems all day. Even a brief break from low thoughts can bring relief.

Different Types of Activity

You do not need to do one type of exercise. Find what works best for your body, your interests, and your daily life. Here are a few ideas:

1. **Walking**
   Walking is simple and free. You can do it almost anywhere—around your neighborhood, on a treadmill if you have access to a gym, or even in a park. Start slow. Maybe a 10-minute walk feels right. Over time, you can build up to 15 or 20 minutes. If it is too hot or cold outside, look for indoor walking areas like a hallway or mall (if that is available).
2. **Dancing**
   Dancing can be done alone in your room with music you like. It can also be done in a class if you feel up to joining a group. It is a fun way to get your body moving, and you can choose the style that you enjoy—slow and gentle, or fast and lively.
3. **Yoga or Stretching**
   These activities focus on gentle movements and can improve balance and flexibility. Many people find them calming. You can look for free videos or classes online. If you are a

beginner, stick to simple poses. Over time, you may feel less tension in your body.

4. **Light Strength Work**
   You do not need heavy weights or complicated machines. Simple bodyweight exercises, like squats or push-ups against a wall, can help you feel stronger. Resistance bands are another option if you want to add a bit of tension without lifting heavy weights.
5. **Team Sports**
   If you enjoy social contact, joining a casual sports group can combine exercise with making friends. This might be a local basketball club or a soccer team. The fun of playing in a group can help distract from sadness.
6. **Household Tasks**
   Tasks like cleaning, gardening, or raking leaves can also count as activity. If you do not want a structured workout, doing chores can still get your body moving. You can make it more fun by playing music while you do them.
7. **Swimming**
   If you have access to a pool or a safe swimming spot, this is a gentle way to move because the water supports your body weight. It can be especially good if your joints ache, as water reduces the impact on them.

Overcoming Low Energy

When you feel very down, the hardest part can be getting started. Here are ways to manage that:

1. **Set Small Goals**
   Instead of saying, "I will exercise for 30 minutes," start with 5 or 10 minutes. Tell yourself you only need to do it for that short time. Often, after you start, you might find you can keep going a bit longer.

2. **Schedule It**
   Pick a time of day that tends to be easier for you. It might be mid-morning if you feel a little more awake, or early evening if that is when you usually have a small burst of energy. Put it in a planner or set an alarm on your phone. Having a set time can lower the chance of pushing it off.
3. **Pair It With Something Enjoyable**
   Listen to an audiobook or some calm music while walking. Watch a funny video or show if you have access to a treadmill. This can help you link the activity with a pleasant experience.
4. **Ask for Support**
   If you have a friend or family member who also wants to move more, try doing it together. You can keep each other on track. Having someone waiting for you can make it less tempting to skip a planned activity.
5. **Track Progress**
   You can write down how many minutes you moved or how you felt afterward. Even a quick note like "walked 10 minutes, felt a bit calmer" can remind you that the effort made some difference. This can help you stay motivated.

Exercising Safely

1. **Check With a Doctor**
   If you have health issues or you have not exercised in a long time, consider talking to a doctor first. They can advise on what level of activity is safe for you.
2. **Warm Up and Cool Down**
   Before starting any activity, do some gentle arm circles or leg swings to warm up your muscles. After you finish, take a few minutes to stretch lightly or walk slowly. This helps protect against injuries.

3. **Listen to Your Body**
   If something hurts in a sharp or concerning way, stop or slow down. A little muscle soreness the next day can be normal if you are using muscles you have not used much. But severe pain is a sign to rest or seek advice.
4. **Stay Hydrated**
   Drink water before, during, and after physical activity. Dehydration can lead to headaches or fatigue, which can make you feel even lower.
5. **Dress Comfortably**
   Wear clothes and shoes that fit well and allow movement. Avoid items that cause discomfort or restrict you. If you are outdoors, consider the weather—dress warmly when it is cold and choose cool, breathable fabrics in the heat.

Making Activity a Habit

1. **Start Slow**
   Doing too much too soon can burn you out, both physically and mentally. Begin with an amount of movement that feels manageable. Over time, increase the duration or intensity slightly.
2. **Set Clear but Flexible Goals**
   You might aim to walk three days a week for 15 minutes. If you manage to do 20 minutes one day, that is a bonus. If you only do 10 on another day, that is still something. The key is to keep it consistent.
3. **Plan for Setbacks**
   Life can interfere. You might get sick or have a tough week at school or work. You might feel especially down some days. It is okay to skip an activity if it truly feels too much. The goal is to return to it when possible.
4. **Reward Yourself**
   After you complete a week of sticking to your plan, do

something nice for yourself (that is not harmful, like a small treat or a relaxing bath). This can help reinforce the habit. It does not have to be big or expensive.

5. **Change It Up**
Doing the same exercise every time can become boring. Try different activities if you are able, like walking one day and gentle stretching the next. A bit of variety can keep you interested.

Overcoming Barriers

1. **Lack of Time**
If your schedule is tight, see if you can fit in 5 or 10 minutes of movement at different points in the day—maybe a quick break to walk around the block or do some stretches. Small segments can add up.
2. **Feeling Too Tired**
It may seem strange, but gentle exercise can actually boost your energy over time. Start with the simplest option—maybe walk in place for a minute or two. If you truly cannot manage more, try again the next day. Over time, being active may reduce that constant tiredness.
3. **Self-Consciousness**
Some people feel shy about working out in front of others, especially if they worry about how they look. If this is the case, try home-based options first. You can find online videos to guide you. Or walk in a quieter area if possible.
4. **Physical Limits**
Not everyone can do high-impact activities. If you have pain or an injury, choose low-impact options like swimming or stationary cycling if possible. If you use a wheelchair, there are seated exercises you can do to work your upper body.
5. **Mental Blocks**
Depression might tell you it is pointless. It might say you will

never feel better, so why bother? Remember that these thoughts are part of the condition. Even if it feels pointless, a small amount of activity can still offer a slight lift. Over time, it can add up to a noticeable change.

Social and Outdoor Options

1. **Walks in Nature**
   If safe and available, going to a park or nature area can help you relax. Greenery or water can calm the mind. The fresh air can also help you think more clearly.
2. **Group Classes**
   If you feel up to being around others, a gentle group fitness class can offer both movement and social contact. This might be a beginner yoga class or a dance class.
3. **Play with Pets**
   If you have a dog, taking them for a walk can be a good way to make activity fun. Even playing fetch or tug-of-war with a pet can get your body moving. If you do not have a pet but enjoy animals, some shelters allow volunteers to walk dogs.
4. **Community Sports**
   Some neighborhoods have casual sports leagues where people of all skill levels are welcome. They often focus on having a good time rather than strict competition.

Linking Activity to Mood Tracking

You can use a simple note or a journal to record how you feel before and after movement. Jot down:

- **Type of Activity** (walk, stretch, etc.)
- **Length of Time** (10 minutes, 20 minutes)

- **How You Felt Before** (tired, sad, anxious)
- **How You Felt After** (slightly better, calmer, still tired but a bit relieved)

Over several weeks, you might see a pattern: perhaps you notice that walking in the morning leaves you a bit more awake for the rest of the day. Or maybe stretching in the evening helps you sleep better. This information can help you tailor your routine to what works best.

Seeking Professional Guidance

If you want a more structured approach or have health concerns:

1. **Physical Therapist**
   A physical therapist can create a tailored plan if you have injuries or physical conditions. They can suggest specific exercises that support your joints and reduce pain.
2. **Certified Trainer**
   If you can afford it or find a free program, a trainer can show you safe exercise methods and help you set goals. Look for someone who understands mental health challenges.
3. **Doctor's Input**
   If you are worried about your heart or any medical issue, ask your doctor what levels of activity are safe for you. They can also guide you on how to pace yourself.

Encouraging Yourself

When depression is loud in your mind, it can say things like, "This will not help. Why bother?" A helpful response might be, "I understand I feel this way, but I will try it for just a few minutes anyway." Remind yourself that even if it does not solve everything, it might make the rest of the day a bit easier. Each small step is still a step forward, no matter how small it seems.

If you do manage a small workout or a short walk, take a moment to note that you took care of yourself in that way. You might feel no burst of joy, but at least you did something good for your body and mind. Over time, the repeated effort can add up.

Long-Term Benefits

1. **Steadier Moods**
   Regular activity can lead to fewer severe dips in mood. It might not remove sadness fully, but it can lower the intensity or duration of your low times.
2. **Healthy Body**
   An active lifestyle supports your heart, muscles, and lungs. Even if you are only doing gentle work, your body can get stronger and more resilient.
3. **Possible Social Connections**
   If you pick group activities, you might make new friends or at least get some friendly interaction. This can help reduce feelings of isolation that often come with depression.
4. **Better Focus**
   Moving your body can help clear mental fog. You may find it easier to focus on tasks after an exercise session, whether it is writing a paper or doing chores.

Remembering Your Unique Pace

Everyone's body is different. Some might find they can do a 30-minute walk with no trouble, while others get tired after 5 minutes. That is okay. Depression also varies from person to person. On some days, you may be able to do more, and on other days, you might do less. Comparing yourself to others can be unhelpful. Instead, measure your progress by your own baseline.

If you used to be active and then stopped because of low mood, it can be frustrating to see how much strength or endurance you lost. Rather than feeling defeated, gently start again. Celebrate each small bit of strength you gain back. If you were never active before, try to see this as an opportunity to learn what your body can do. Even small efforts can lead to feeling a bit stronger over time.

Putting It All Together

Moving your body is not just about trying to be in shape. It is a tool you can use to help manage sad or anxious feelings. Even modest activity can help you feel a bit more stable. You can start by simply standing up and walking around the room, then progress to longer or different types of movement. There is no deadline. Take your time, try different things, and see what fits you best.

Remember to keep safety in mind, listen to your body, and allow for ups and downs. If you miss a day or a week, that does not mean you failed. It means you are human. Try again when you can. Over time, you might find that having some movement in your routine helps you feel more balanced, both physically and mentally.

In the next chapter, we will talk about ways to calm a restless or busy mind. Sometimes, even if you move your body, your thoughts may still race or get stuck on sadness. Learning how to quiet the mind can offer another layer of support. Combine physical activity with mind-calming methods for the most benefit. With these tools, you can build a stronger foundation for handling depressed feelings and move toward feeling more at ease.

Chapter 8: Quieting the Mind

Sadness can feel overwhelming when it fills your thoughts day after day. Negative ideas might loop through your mind, making it hard to focus on anything else. Quieting the mind does not mean forcing yourself to stop thinking altogether. Instead, it is about finding ways to bring calm and reduce mental noise. This chapter explores various methods to settle racing thoughts, ease worry, and help you feel calmer on the inside.

Why a Restful Mind Matters

1. **Less Overwhelm**
   When your mind is constantly busy with sad or anxious thoughts, everyday tasks feel harder. Calming your thoughts can make these tasks more approachable. You have more mental energy to handle school, work, or personal issues.
2. **Improved Sleep**
   Racing thoughts often keep people awake at night. By learning techniques to slow those thoughts, you may find it easier to relax and rest.
3. **Reduced Stress in the Body**
   Your mind and body are linked. When your brain is stressed, your body can tense up. Muscles get tight, and headaches or stomach troubles can happen. Calming the mind can ease these physical issues.
4. **Better Mood**
   Constant negative thinking can worsen sadness. Finding moments of mental quiet, even brief ones, can lift some of that heaviness. Over time, regular calming practices can lead to a steadier mood overall.

Simple Breathing Methods

1. **Deep Breathing**
   - **How**: Inhale slowly through your nose for a count of four, hold for a moment, then exhale through your mouth for a count of four.
   - **Why**: This sends a message to your nervous system to relax. It slows your heart rate and can reduce feelings of panic.
2. **Box Breathing**
   - **How**: Breathe in through your nose for four seconds, hold for four seconds, breathe out through your mouth for four seconds, hold for four seconds again, and repeat.
   - **Why**: The structured rhythm helps you focus on the process rather than on stressful thoughts.
3. **Extended Exhale**
   - **How**: Breathe in for a count of four and out for a count of six or eight.
   - **Why**: Lengthening the exhale can calm your body and is often used during stress to bring fast relief.
4. **Mindful Notice**
   - **How**: Simply notice your breath without trying to change it. Observe how the air feels as it enters your nose and travels down, then leaves again.
   - **Why**: Focusing on the natural process of breathing helps ground you in the present moment.

Guided Imagery

1. **Peaceful Place**
   - **What**: Picture a setting that brings you comfort—maybe a quiet beach, a soft forest, or a cozy

room. Try to include details like smells, colors, and sounds.
    - **How**: Sit or lie down, close your eyes, and slowly build this scene in your mind. Spend a few minutes there, noticing each detail.
2. **Safe Spot**
    - **What**: Imagine a spot where you feel protected. It might be a warm blanket fort or a quiet garden.
    - **How**: When your mind is stormy, close your eyes and bring up this image. Stay there until you feel a bit calmer.

Guided imagery is not about escaping reality forever. It is a short mental retreat that can ease racing thoughts. Once you feel calmer, you can approach your real-world tasks with a clearer head.

Progressive Muscle Relaxation

1. **Tensing and Releasing**
    - **How**: Lie down or sit comfortably. Start at your toes—tense them for a few seconds, then let go. Move up to your calves, thighs, belly, hands, arms, shoulders, and so on.
    - **Why**: By systematically tightening and then releasing muscles, you learn to spot tension and how it feels to relax them. This method can also distract the mind from negative thoughts.
2. **Guided Audio**
    - **Option**: Look for audio tracks or short online videos that walk you through muscle relaxation. They can help you stay on track and keep a steady pace.

Mindful Observation

1. **Using the Senses**
   - **How**: Sit quietly and notice what you see, hear, smell, feel, or taste. You do not have to label them good or bad. Just notice.
   - **Why**: Grounding in the present can stop your mind from running in circles about the past or future.
2. **Everyday Objects**
   - **How**: Pick an object, like a pencil or a leaf, and study it for a minute. Notice its shape, texture, color.
   - **Why**: This simple focus can give your mind a break from worries. It trains you to pay attention to details right in front of you.

Journaling for Calm

1. **Free Write**
   - **How**: Set a timer for 5 or 10 minutes and write whatever comes to mind. Do not worry about grammar or spelling. If a negative thought appears, jot it down.
   - **Why**: Releasing thoughts onto paper can feel like clearing out mental clutter. Sometimes seeing your worries in writing makes them less overwhelming.
2. **Positive Statements**
   - **How**: Along with free writing, try to add one or two statements about something that went okay that day. It can be very small, like "I got up on time" or "I had a decent lunch."
   - **Why**: This helps your brain notice that not everything is negative. Over time, this can support a more balanced perspective.
3. **Letters You Never Send**

- **How**: If you are upset with someone or something, write them a letter. Express your feelings honestly. Then put the letter away or discard it.
- **Why**: Getting those emotions out can help you move on without the stress of a confrontation if that is not safe or possible.

Art Activities

1. **Coloring or Drawing**
   - **Why**: Activities that let you focus on shapes and colors can settle your mind. Adult coloring books or simple doodles can work.
   - **How**: Set aside a small window of time, pick a design you like, and color it in. Or draw patterns, scribbles, or anything that feels soothing.
2. **Crafting**
   - **Why**: Making something with your hands, like simple clay objects or paper crafts, can bring you into the present moment.
   - **How**: Choose a basic project. Do not worry about making it perfect. The goal is to gently focus on the process.
3. **Photography**
   - **Why**: Looking for interesting or pretty things to photograph forces you to pay attention to your surroundings.
   - **How**: If you have a camera or a phone, try taking pictures of small details around you—a flower, a cloud shape, or a pattern on a sidewalk.

Quiet Moments During the Day

1. **Short Pauses**
   - **How**: If your day is busy, try to take tiny breaks. Close your eyes for 10 seconds and take a slow breath or two.
   - **Why**: These mini-pauses can interrupt a stream of stressful thoughts. They remind you to slow down.
2. **Break from Noise**
   - **How**: If possible, switch off your phone and other devices for a few minutes. Sit quietly or step outside if it is safe.
   - **Why**: Constant noise from messages or social media can keep your brain buzzing. Short breaks can help you breathe and refocus.
3. **Relaxing Music**
   - **How**: Pick music with a calm tempo and low volume. Sit or lie down and just listen.
   - **Why**: Gentle music can help the mind settle. Some people prefer nature sounds, like ocean waves or rain.

Thinking Patterns and Replacing Them

1. **Identify Negative Thoughts**
   - **How**: When you catch yourself thinking a negative thought, write it down.
   - **Example**: "I am worthless."
   - **Why**: Recognizing a negative thought is the first step in managing it.
2. **Question the Thought**
   - **How**: Ask yourself, "Is this always true? Is there any evidence against this?"
   - **Example**: "Would I say this to a friend who is going through a hard time?"

- **Why**: Many negative thoughts are not fully accurate. Questioning them can loosen their power.
3. **Replace It with a More Balanced View**
    - **How**: Find a statement that is more realistic or kinder.
    - **Example**: "I am trying my best. I have done good things before."
    - **Why**: You are not lying to yourself; you are recognizing that the original thought might be too harsh. A balanced view can bring a calmer mindset.

Relaxation Apps and Tools

1. **Calming Apps**
    - **What**: Many apps offer guided breathing, meditation, or relaxation exercises.
    - **Tip**: Try free versions first to see if you like them. Some provide short sessions that fit easily into your day.
2. **White Noise Machines**
    - **What**: Devices or apps that play consistent sounds (like a fan or gentle rain) to help block out distractions.
    - **Why**: If you find random noises stressful, white noise can help you relax or focus on a calmer sound.
3. **Timer and Reminders**
    - **How**: Use your phone or a clock to set reminders for relaxation breaks.
    - **Why**: It is easy to forget to take mental breaks when you are busy or feeling low.

Quieting the Mind at Night

1. **Pre-Bed Routine**
   - **How**: About an hour before bedtime, turn off bright screens or reduce screen time if possible. Do a quiet activity—reading a gentle book, light stretches, or listening to soft music.
   - **Why**: This signals your brain that it is time to relax. It can make falling asleep easier.
2. **Gratitude Notes**
   - **How**: Write down one or two small things you appreciated that day. It might be a friendly text from someone or a nice meal.
   - **Why**: Ending the day with this action can shift your mind away from negative thoughts.
3. **Body Scan**
   - **How**: Lie in bed, starting at your toes and moving up to your head. Notice each part of your body and try to relax it.
   - **Why**: Focusing on different areas of your body can keep your mind from wandering into anxious thoughts.
4. **If You Cannot Sleep**
   - **How**: After about 20 minutes of trying, if you are still wide awake, get up and do something calm in dim light—like reading or gentle stretching. Then try to go back to bed.
   - **Why**: Lying in bed stressed can teach your brain to see the bed as a place of worry. Doing a quiet activity can help reset this.

Common Hurdles

1. **"I Cannot Stop My Thoughts"**

- **Response**: It is normal to have thoughts. The aim is not to remove them entirely, but to guide them toward calmer patterns or let them pass without latching on.
2. **"I Feel Silly Doing These Exercises"**
    - **Response**: Trying something new can feel odd. Remind yourself that you are doing this for your well-being. Over time, it may feel more natural.
3. **"No Time for Relaxation"**
    - **Response**: Short breaks can be as little as 30 seconds or 1 minute. Even a quick pause can bring some relief. You do not need an hour-long session.
4. **"I Tried Once, and It Did Not Work"**
    - **Response**: Quieting the mind takes practice. Like learning an instrument, it might not show big results immediately. Stick with it for a week or two and see if you notice changes.

Combining Quiet Mind Methods with Other Support

1. **Therapy**
    - **How**: Therapists can teach more methods to manage thoughts. They can guide you through deeper relaxation techniques and help you handle the roots of sadness.
    - **Why**: Professional input can speed up progress and give you personalized ideas.
2. **Medication**
    - **How**: Some medications can help balance brain chemicals if you have ongoing depression or anxiety.
    - **Why**: Medication does not replace mind-calming exercises, but it can make it easier to use them effectively by lowering the intensity of negative feelings.
3. **Routine Adjustments**

- **How**: Carve out time in the morning or evening for mind-quieting. Maybe just five or ten minutes.
- **Why**: Placing these methods into a regular routine can make them a normal part of your day rather than an afterthought.
4. **Physical Activity**
    - **How**: You can pair a quieting method with a short walk or gentle stretching. For instance, do a breathing exercise right after a walk.
    - **Why**: Movement can burn off extra tension, and then relaxation techniques can deepen the calm.

Signs of Progress

Quieting the mind is not about never feeling sad or never having a tough day. Look for small signs that you are building a calmer mindset:

- You notice that when a negative thought arises, you can pause and question it instead of instantly believing it.
- You remember to breathe deeply during a stressful moment, and it helps you feel a bit more in control.
- You find that your body does not feel as tense as it used to.
- You catch yourself being a little more patient with everyday frustrations.

These are signs that your practice is taking hold. They might be subtle at first, so give yourself time to see these shifts.

Keeping It Going

1. **Pick a Few Techniques**
You do not need to do everything. Maybe you like deep

breathing and journaling. Focus on those. If you get bored or they stop helping, try another approach.
2. **Set Realistic Expectations**
If you expect all your sad thoughts to vanish overnight, you might feel disappointed. Aim for small, gradual changes. Each time you calm your mind, you give yourself a little more room to breathe.
3. **Share with Supportive People**
If you have a friend or family member who is also dealing with stress, you can practice certain methods together. Or you can talk about your experiences and learn from each other.
4. **Adapt to Life Changes**
If you move to a new place or your schedule shifts, you might need to tweak your methods. The key is to stay flexible. A short breathing exercise can fit almost any routine if you decide to make time for it.

Putting It All Into Practice

Start with one approach—maybe deep breathing:

1. **When**: Before you get out of bed in the morning and once before you go to sleep at night.
2. **How Long**: Aim for a minute or two at first.
3. **Next Step**: If it helps, you could try guided imagery on top of that. Maybe once a day, you imagine a peaceful place for a few minutes.

Notice how you feel over a week or two. Do you feel a tiny bit calmer at some points? Is it easier to handle small tasks? If so, keep going and explore more methods. If not, try a different approach—maybe journaling or muscle relaxation—until you find something that resonates.

Chapter 9: Shifting Negative Thoughts

It is very common for someone facing deep sadness to have negative ideas running through their mind. These ideas can focus on fears about the future, regrets about the past, or a sense of hopelessness about the present. Sometimes, the voice in your head might say harsh things like, "I am not good enough" or, "Things will never improve." Shifting such thoughts is not about denying the real problems in life. Rather, it is about noticing when these thinking patterns become harmful and learning ways to counter them with more balanced, fair thoughts. In this chapter, we will look at how negative thoughts appear, why they are so convincing, and what can be done to change them little by little.

Why Do Negative Thoughts Appear?

1. **Sense of Protection**
   Our brains are wired to notice problems or dangers. In a situation where there is a real threat, noticing it quickly can help you stay safe. However, when sadness or anxiety is high, the mind may see threats everywhere, including situations that pose no real danger. This can lead to a constant stream of negative thoughts.
2. **Prior Hurt**
   If you have faced repeated setbacks—like losing friends, failing tests, or being put down by others—your mind might start expecting the worst. It might believe that getting hurt again is certain. This defensive stance can become a habit, shaping your thoughts in a negative direction.
3. **Chemical Factors**
   Depression can involve imbalances in the brain's chemistry. These imbalances can lower your mood and affect the way you think. Even if there is no clear outside cause, you might

find yourself having harsh thoughts about yourself or the future.

4. **Fear of Disappointment**
   Sometimes, people think negatively because they want to avoid feeling disappointed. They might believe that by expecting the worst, they protect themselves from shock or pain. However, this pattern can lock them in a cycle of ongoing gloom.

Recognizing Harmful Thought Patterns

You might wonder, "How do I know if my thinking is negative or if I am just being realistic?" Here are some signs that your thought patterns could be harmful:

1. **All-or-Nothing Thinking**
   Seeing things as all good or all bad, with no middle ground. For example, telling yourself, "I made one mistake, so I am a total failure," ignores all the times you have done things right.
2. **Overgeneralizing**
   Drawing a sweeping conclusion from a single event. Maybe you had one argument with a friend and now believe, "Nobody will ever like me." That is an overgeneralization that goes beyond the facts.
3. **Focusing Only on the Negative**
   This is also called a mental filter. You might pick out a single negative detail from a situation and dwell on it, ignoring anything that went well. For example, you get praise on a project, but one person gives you mild feedback, and you dwell on that only.
4. **Jumping to Worst Conclusions**
   Also known as catastrophizing. If you feel a small ache, you assume it must be something severe. If a friend does not text back quickly, you decide they must hate you now.

5. **Discounting the Positive**
   If something good happens, you might say it is just luck or that it does not count for real. This keeps you from letting any positive fact in, feeding the negative cycle.
6. **Self-Blame**
   You blame yourself for things that are not fully your fault. You may feel like you carry the burden of everything that goes wrong, even if it is out of your control.

How Negative Thinking Feeds Sadness

Negative thoughts can become a cycle:

- **Sadness or Worry Emerges**: Something triggers a low mood or anxious feeling.
- **Negative Thoughts Appear**: You might think, "I always mess up," or, "No one would ever care about me."
- **Worsening Mood**: Those thoughts produce more sadness, shame, or anger.
- **Less Motivation**: When your mood is worse, you might skip helpful actions, like talking to a friend or going for a short walk.
- **Ongoing Low Feelings**: The lack of positive action leads to more negative thoughts.

Breaking this loop means challenging the negative thoughts that appear and making room for more balanced and realistic ideas. This does not mean forcing cheerfulness or ignoring real problems. It means treating your thoughts like statements that can be questioned rather than absolute truths.

Methods to Shift Negative Thoughts

1. **Thought-Checking**
   - **Step 1**: Notice a negative thought when it pops up. For example, "I will never succeed."
   - **Step 2**: Ask, "Is there evidence that this statement is always true?" Look for facts that show it might not be.
   - **Step 3**: Replace it with a more balanced statement. For instance, "There have been times I succeeded in smaller tasks, so it is not true that I never succeed."
2. **Writing Thought Records**
   - **How It Works**: When a harsh thought enters your mind, write down the situation, your feelings, and the thought. Then write down any facts that support that thought and any facts that go against it.
   - **Benefit**: Seeing your thoughts on paper can help you notice that they are not always 100% accurate. It gives you a chance to come up with a statement that is kinder or more neutral.
3. **Questioning Words Like "Always" and "Never"**
   - **Example**: If you say, "I never do anything right," ask yourself, "Is that true? Have I truly never done anything right?"
   - **Why It Helps**: "Always" and "never" statements are usually too broad. Finding even one exception breaks that extreme thinking.
4. **Posing as a Friend to Yourself**
   - **Technique**: Imagine a close friend is telling you about their negative thoughts. Would you say to them, "Yes, you are worthless"? Probably not. You would likely point out their good qualities.
   - **Outcome**: By treating yourself like a friend, you might find more gentle ways of seeing the situation.
5. **Mindful Redirection**

- **Process**: When a painful thought arises, gently notice it, but do not let it fully take over. You can say to yourself, "I see this thought, but I do not have to follow it."
- **Example**: Imagine the thought as a train passing by. You can watch it without hopping on board. This helps you gain some distance from the negativity.

Building Helpful Inner Dialogue

1. **Use Neutral or Positive Words**
    - Instead of saying "I messed up, I am so dumb," try something like, "I made a mistake, but I can learn from it."
    - This does not mean lying to yourself. It is about reducing the blow of harsh wording.
2. **Practice Acknowledging Effort**
    - Even if an outcome was not perfect, notice the fact that you tried or put in some effort. For example, say, "I tried to study an extra 30 minutes last night. That shows I am making an attempt."
3. **Find Small Accomplishments**
    - Each day, see if there is one small thing that went okay. Perhaps you got out of bed on time, or you managed to finish a certain chore. Remind yourself, "I managed that, so I am not a total failure."
4. **Avoid Over-Apologizing**
    - Negative thinking might cause you to say "sorry" too often, even for things that are not your fault. Be careful to only say sorry when you have truly done something to apologize for. This helps prevent excessive blame and guilt.

Changing the Environment for Better Thinking

Sometimes, shifting negative thoughts requires more than just mental exercises. Changing aspects of your surroundings can help as well:

1. **Limit Overexposure to Bad News**
   - If you find that reading negative headlines or scrolling through upsetting social media posts brings on gloom, give yourself boundaries. Maybe set a time limit or avoid certain platforms altogether.
2. **Spend Time in Calmer Spaces**
   - If your home environment is chaotic or always noisy, see if you can find a quieter spot—a library, a park, or a corner of your room. A calm environment can make it easier to notice and counter negative thoughts.
3. **Use Reminders**
   - Small notes on your phone or sticky notes on your mirror that say things like, "Check your thoughts" or "Speak kindly to yourself" can spark you to pause when negativity creeps in.
4. **Seek Healthy Interactions**
   - Surround yourself, if possible, with people who are gentle and understanding. Listening to constant criticism from others can reinforce your own harsh thoughts.

Handling Persistent Negative Thoughts

Even when you practice these methods, some negative thoughts might keep returning. Here are ways to handle that:

1. **Accept That Thoughts Are Not Facts**

- A thought in your mind is not always true. It can be a reaction to stress or past hurt. Just because you think something does not make it a fact.
2. **Schedule a "Worry Time"**
    - This might sound strange, but some people find it helpful to set aside a few minutes each day (maybe late afternoon) to allow worries. If a worry pops up at other times, remind yourself you will deal with it at your "worry time." This can prevent all-day rumination.
3. **Seek Professional Help**
    - If negative thoughts are too heavy and do not let up despite your best efforts, a counselor or therapist can guide you through more structured approaches (like cognitive behavioral therapy). They can show you detailed strategies to identify and shift unhelpful thinking.
4. **Keep a Longer-Term View**
    - Realizing that shifting negative thoughts is a process helps manage frustration. You are training your brain in new habits. Habits take time to build.

Finding Balanced Views

Sometimes, people think that being balanced means everything is magically good. It is more about seeing both the difficulties and the possibilities. For instance:

- **Harsh Thought**: "I am a horrible person because I said something rude."
- **Balanced Thought**: "I made a mistake, and I feel sorry about it. I can apologize and try to do better next time."

Balanced thinking recognizes mistakes but does not define your entire worth by them. It gives you room to learn or improve without extreme self-judgment.

Activities That Can Support Healthier Thoughts

1. **Reading Uplifting Content**
   - This does not mean ignoring real issues in life. But reading books or articles that offer positive, realistic perspectives can shift your mindset from constant negativity.
2. **Volunteering or Helping Others**
   - Taking part in a local charity or helping a family member can remind you that you have value and can do good things. Such actions often fight the notion of worthlessness.
3. **Music or Storytelling**
   - Listening to songs with thoughtful or encouraging lyrics can place new, more positive ideas in your head. Similarly, hearing stories where characters face challenges but find hope can help you see that adversity does not always end badly.
4. **Limit Comparison**
   - Comparing yourself to others—like noticing people on social media who seem to have perfect lives—can feed negative thoughts. Remember that social media often shows only the best parts of people's lives. Reducing this habit may help calm your own mind.

Taking Stock of Progress

After a few weeks of trying to shift negative thoughts, check if you see small changes. Ask yourself:

- Are the thoughts arriving less often, or do they have slightly less power?
- Can I now pause and question them before fully believing them?
- Do I feel a tiny bit more hopeful about certain aspects of life?

Even if the improvement is small, it is still an improvement. Over time, these small improvements can add up, giving you more mental and emotional space to deal with real problems in a clearer way.

Common Pitfalls and How to Address Them

1. **Expecting Instant Results**
   - Switching long-standing thought patterns does not happen in one day. If you feel discouraged, remind yourself that you are learning a new skill. With repeated practice, it can get easier.
2. **Replacing Negativity with Blind Optimism**
   - Telling yourself everything is perfect can feel fake. Balanced thinking means acknowledging both good and bad, finding realistic hope in the middle.
3. **Giving Up After a Bad Day**
   - You might do well for a while, then have a day where negative thoughts flood back. That does not mean you failed. It is normal to have ups and downs. Keep going with the skills you have learned.
4. **Letting Others Drag You Down**
   - If certain people around you constantly speak harshly, it can feed your negative mindset. You might need to limit your contact or set boundaries if possible.

Pairing Thought Shifts with Other Supports

Remember, shifting negative thoughts is one piece of improving your well-being. It pairs well with:

- **Healthy Routines**: Having structure in your day (see Chapter 5) can reduce chaos that leads to negative thinking.
- **Physical Activity**: A simple walk or stretch (Chapter 7) can make you feel less anxious, which supports clearer thinking.
- **Quieting the Mind**: Practices from Chapter 8 can help calm your mental chatter, allowing you space to question negative thoughts.
- **Supportive Relationships**: Talking to kind friends (Chapter 4) can provide outside perspectives that challenge your negative self-view.

Together, these approaches offer multiple pathways to feeling better.

Planning a Thought-Shifting Routine

It might help to create a small plan for your day that includes checking your thoughts:

1. **Morning Check**
   - Upon waking, note any immediate negative thoughts. Gently question them. This sets a tone for the day.
2. **Afternoon Reminder**
   - Place an alarm on your phone to go off once, maybe after lunch. When it rings, pause and consider if you have been stuck in negative thinking. Do a quick thought-check if needed.
3. **Evening Reflection**

- Write down one or two negative thoughts you had that day, plus a balanced replacement for each. Over time, this can reduce how often those thoughts return.
4. **Keep It Manageable**
    - You do not need to spend hours on this. Even 5 minutes here and there can train your mind to become aware of unhelpful thoughts.

A Gentle Example

Let us consider a short scenario: Sam has been feeling very down. Sam thinks, "I am worthless at school." By noticing this thought, Sam might say:

- **What triggered it?**
  "I did badly on one math test."
- **Is that always true?**
  "I have done well in some other subjects, and not all of my math scores are bad."
- **What could be more balanced?**
  "I am struggling with math right now, but that does not make me worthless. I can try a different study method or ask for help."

With this shift, Sam may not instantly feel great, but the hopeless finality of "I am worthless" becomes less convincing. Sam sees that there are options, such as seeking a tutor or talking to the teacher. This small change in perspective can open the door to solutions.

Chapter 10: Planning Tasks

Feeling overwhelmed is a common part of deep sadness. When you are down, even small tasks—like washing dishes or replying to emails—can seem huge. This can lead to procrastination, missing deadlines, or letting chores build up until they feel unmanageable. Learning to plan tasks in a simple, step-by-step way can help you avoid this stress. By mapping out what needs to be done and breaking it into smaller parts, you can reduce anxiety and give yourself a sense of achievement as you check items off. In this chapter, we will explore how to set priorities, make realistic goals, and handle both big and small tasks in a calmer way.

Why Task Planning Matters

1. **Reduces Mental Overload**
   Trying to remember everything in your head can be draining. Writing tasks down or using a planner takes that load off your mind. This can help you feel more in control and less frazzled.
2. **Breaks Through Avoidance**
   Depression often leads to putting tasks off. Clear planning can help you see that even if a task feels large, it can be tackled in smaller steps. This lowers the feeling of being stuck.
3. **Builds Self-Trust**
   Each time you complete a task on your plan, you remind yourself that you can take action, even if your mood is not great. This can push back against negative thoughts like "I cannot do anything right."
4. **Prevents Last-Minute Stress**
   When you have a plan, you are less likely to wake up one day and realize a big assignment is due in a few hours. You can

pace your work so that you have fewer surprises and less panic.

Sorting Tasks by Priority

1. **Must-Do Tasks**
   These are tasks that must be done soon to avoid negative outcomes. They might include paying a bill before a deadline, submitting a school assignment, or attending a necessary appointment. Put these at the top of your list.
2. **Should-Do Tasks**
   These are tasks that are important but may have flexible deadlines. For instance, cleaning your room or organizing a closet. It is good to do them, but they may not lead to an immediate crisis if delayed.
3. **Nice-to-Do Tasks**
   These are tasks that can bring some benefit or joy, but are not urgent. Examples might include learning a new hobby or rearranging your bookshelves. They can be done once you have handled higher priority items.
4. **Daily Living Tasks**
   Tasks like taking a shower, brushing your teeth, or making the bed might be very basic, but when you are depressed, even these can require planning. It can help to list them if you find yourself skipping them or feeling too tired.

Making a Task List or Planner

1. **Pick a Format**
   - Some like paper planners; others prefer phone apps or computer spreadsheets. Choose what feels easiest for you.

- Make it something you can check often. If you rarely use paper, a phone app might be better, and vice versa.
2. **List Everything First**
    - Write down all the tasks you can think of, no matter how small. This might include finishing homework, buying groceries, or calling the doctor.
    - Getting them out of your head and onto paper (or a screen) can bring relief right away.
3. **Sort by Priority and Deadline**
    - Ask yourself: Which tasks need to happen today? Tomorrow? Next week?
    - Put due dates if they exist. That helps you see which tasks must be handled first.
4. **Keep It Manageable**
    - If you have a very long list, it can look overwhelming. Group similar tasks together (like all the phone calls you need to make). Or, highlight the top three for today so you know where to start.

Breaking Tasks into Steps

One reason tasks feel scary is that we see them as one giant thing to do. Breaking them down can ease that pressure:

1. **Example: Writing a School Essay**
    - Break it into smaller parts:
        1. Choose a topic.
        2. Gather research.
        3. Make an outline.
        4. Write a first draft.
        5. Edit and proofread.
    - If you see it as separate steps, it is less daunting than saying, "Write the whole paper."

2. **Example: Cleaning Your Room**
   - Divide it into mini-tasks:
     1. Throw away trash.
     2. Sort dirty clothes and start a laundry load.
     3. Put books or papers in their place.
     4. Wipe surfaces.
     5. Vacuum or sweep.
   - You can do one or two of these steps at a time, rather than everything at once.
3. **Tracking Progress**
   - After you finish a small step, you can mark it off. This creates a feeling of moving forward. Even if the entire project is not done, you see that you have completed part of it.

Creating Time Blocks

1. **What Is a Time Block?**
   - A time block means setting aside a specific period for a task or group of tasks. For example, you could say, "From 2 p.m. to 3 p.m., I will work on my math homework."
2. **Why It Helps**
   - Having a clear start and end time can reduce procrastination. You tell yourself, "I only need to focus on this for one hour," rather than feeling it could take forever.
3. **Be Realistic**
   - If you have trouble focusing for long periods, pick shorter time blocks (20-30 minutes) with short breaks in between. Over time, you can see if you can handle slightly longer blocks.
4. **Use Alarms or Timers**

- You might set a timer for your chosen work period. When the timer goes off, you can take a small break or move on to a new task. This structure can help when you feel scattered.

Dealing with Lack of Motivation

1. **Start with the Easiest Task**
    - Sometimes, picking a small, easy task helps you build momentum. It can lift your mood a bit to realize you can finish something. Then you might feel more able to tackle a bigger task.
2. **Reward Yourself in Simple Ways**
    - For instance, after you complete a difficult task, allow yourself a short break to do something you find pleasant, like listening to a favorite song.
3. **Pair Boring Tasks with Something Pleasant**
    - If you have to fold laundry, you could listen to a calming podcast. If you need to organize your closet, you could play gentle background music. This makes chores less dull.
4. **Use the "5-Minute Rule"**
    - Tell yourself you only have to do a task for 5 minutes. After that, you can stop if you really want to. Often, once you start, you might keep going a bit longer.

Coping with Distractions

1. **Phone Limits**
    - Put your phone on silent, or place it in another room if possible. Scrolling social media can quickly eat away at your focus.

2. **Separate Workspace**
   - If you can, do your tasks in a specific spot—like a desk or table—rather than on your bed. This helps your mind switch into "work mode."
3. **Avoid Multitasking**
   - Studies show multitasking can reduce the quality of your work and increase stress. Stick to one main task at a time, if you can.
4. **Set Boundaries with Others**
   - If you live with family or roommates, let them know when you have set aside time to work on tasks. Ask them not to interrupt unless it is important.

Planning for Breaks

1. **Why Breaks Are Important**
   - Taking a short rest can prevent burnout. It can also give your mind a chance to reset so you can return to your work with better focus.
2. **Short Break Ideas**
   - Stand up and stretch for a minute.
   - Get a drink of water.
   - Take a few deep breaths by a window.
   - Walk around the room or yard.
3. **Longer Breaks**
   - After a couple of hours of steady work, consider a 15- to 20-minute break where you can have a snack or do something relaxing. Be careful not to let a short break extend into losing the whole day if possible.

Handling Big Projects Over Multiple Days

1. **Plan Backwards from the Due Date**
   - If you have a project due in two weeks, break down the tasks needed and spread them out over the days you have. Make sure you leave some buffer time for any unexpected delay.
2. **Check In with Yourself**
   - Each evening (or morning), see how you are doing on your schedule. If you are behind, adjust or set aside extra time to catch up.
3. **Celebrate Finished Parts**
   - When you finish a phase of a big project, acknowledge it. For instance, if you have completed the research part of a report, note that as a positive step forward. (Use care with your wording to avoid certain terms.)
4. **Ask for Help If Overwhelmed**
   - If you find that the project is too large or you keep missing your mini-deadlines, talk to a teacher, coworker, or friend. They might help you plan better or offer assistance.

Making Task Planning a Habit

1. **Daily or Weekly Review**
   - Set aside time each day or week to look over your tasks. You might decide each Sunday to plan the upcoming week. Or each night, you plan the next day.
2. **Keep It Simple**
   - Do not list every single detail of your life in the planner if that overwhelms you. Focus on tasks that truly need planning or feel difficult. With time, you can expand if you want.
3. **Adjust as Needed**

- If your plan is too crowded and you cannot get everything done, learn from that. Try fewer tasks the next day. If your plan is too light, you might add more tasks when you feel ready.
4. **Use Tools Wisely**
    - If you find a to-do list app that syncs across devices, that can be handy. Just be sure you do not spend all your time playing with the app instead of doing tasks. Paper or digital—whatever helps you stay organized is fine.

Overcoming Pitfalls

1. **Perfectionism**
    - Some people avoid tasks because they want them to be done perfectly. Remind yourself that done is better than perfect. You can polish it later if you have time.
    - Setting small milestones helps stop you from freezing at the thought of not doing it flawlessly.
2. **Skipping Tasks That Feel Unpleasant**
    - If you always skip the most uncomfortable tasks, you could create bigger problems. Try to schedule them first or in the morning, so you get them out of the way.
3. **Unrealistic Time Estimates**
    - If you underestimate how long things take, you may end up stressed. Try timing how long certain tasks really take to get a better sense of planning.
4. **Unexpected Interruptions**
    - Life happens—someone might call needing help, or an emergency can arise. If you can, leave a bit of free time in your schedule as a buffer.

Using Task Planning to Support Mental Health

1. **Combines Well with Therapy**
   - Many therapists use methods that include planning tasks as part of treatment for depression or anxiety. It helps you see progress in small steps.
2. **Helps with Routines**
   - Combine your task planning with the healthy routines (Chapter 5) you already have. For example, schedule your morning routine, set times for meals, and then fit tasks around them.
3. **Fights Hopelessness**
   - Depression can make the future seem bleak. A well-structured plan, even for basic chores, gives you a sense of direction. This can lighten the feeling that life is spiraling.
4. **Increases Self-Worth**
   - Checking tasks off your list can give you small but important boosts of confidence. You begin to see that you can accomplish things, even if they are small.

Small Steps for Busy or Bad Days

1. **Focus on One Task**
   - If you have a rough day and cannot handle the full list, try doing just the most necessary item. That might be all you can do. Doing one important thing is better than none.
2. **Micro-Steps**
   - If doing laundry is too much, aim to gather clothes and put them in the basket. If washing dishes is too big, wash a few plates. Sometimes starting small leads to more progress than expected.
3. **Give Yourself Compassion**

- If you cannot complete all the tasks you hoped to do, remember that depression can limit energy. Acknowledge that you are doing what you can. Aim to plan again for the next day, rather than beating yourself up.

Example: A Simple Daily Plan

- **Morning (7 a.m. - 9 a.m.)**
    - Wake up, have breakfast, wash face and brush teeth, take out the trash if it is pick-up day.
- **Late Morning (9 a.m. - 11 a.m.)**
    - Time block for an important task (like studying or finishing a work report).
- **Lunch (12 p.m.)**
    - Make or heat a simple meal.
- **Early Afternoon (1 p.m. - 2 p.m.)**
    - Smaller tasks (replying to emails, paying a bill).
- **Late Afternoon (2 p.m. - 4 p.m.)**
    - Another time block for a different big task (could be a household chore like cleaning a room, or a personal project).
- **Evening (5 p.m. - 6 p.m.)**
    - Prepare dinner, clean up the kitchen, or do a quick walk.
- **Night (7 p.m. - 9 p.m.)**
    - Relaxing activities, time to wind down, read or watch something calm, get ready for bed.

This is just an example. Your schedule may look very different based on your life. The main idea is to keep tasks clear and set aside certain periods for them so you are less likely to feel lost.

Checking Progress and Adjusting

At the end of a day or week, take a look at how well the plan worked:

- **What Tasks Got Done?**
  Acknowledge that you managed to handle them.
- **What Was Missed?**
  See if those missed tasks need to be pushed to tomorrow or next week. Ask yourself if they are still important.
- **How Did You Feel?**
  Notice if planning tasks reduced stress or if it made you feel pressured. Tweak your approach if needed to keep it helpful rather than stressful.

Moving Forward with Planning

Task planning is a skill, and like any skill, it gets easier with practice. At first, it might feel strange or tedious. But each time you sort your tasks, set priorities, and break them into steps, you are teaching your mind to handle responsibilities in a more organized and less stressful way.

In the next chapter, we will discuss improving sleep. A stable plan for your day often helps with sleep quality because you are not lying awake worrying about undone tasks. Combining good task planning with better sleep habits can help you feel more rested, which in turn can boost your ability to keep following your plan and dealing with sadness more effectively.

Keep in mind that some days will be harder than others. That is normal. Give yourself permission to adjust your plans when needed. Over time, planning tasks can become part of your routine, giving you a sense of direction and helping you push through those low moments. By taking it one step at a time, you can make even big tasks feel more manageable, reducing stress and building confidence that you can handle what life throws at you.

Chapter 11: Improving Sleep

When you feel low, sleep can be hard. You might have trouble falling asleep or staying asleep. You might wake up feeling tired even if you spent a lot of time in bed. Good rest is important for your mind and body, so finding ways to sleep better can help ease sadness. In this chapter, we will look at why sleep matters, how lack of rest affects mood, and what you can do to make bedtime calmer. We will cover tips on setting up a good sleep environment, handling restless thoughts, and dealing with nighttime worries in practical ways.

Why Sleep Matters

1. **Body Repair**
   Sleep is when your body does much of its repair work. Cells recover, and muscles and tissues rebuild. If you miss too much sleep, your body cannot perform these tasks as well, which can lead to feeling even more tired and weak the next day.
2. **Mind Recovery**
   While you sleep, your brain processes the day's events and emotions. It helps sort memories and can reduce some mental load. If you are not getting enough sleep, your thoughts may feel tangled. You might wake up feeling stressed or overwhelmed.
3. **Mood Support**
   Lack of sleep can make sadness, anger, or worry feel bigger. Even people without depression can feel crabby if they do not sleep enough. For those already dealing with low mood, poor rest can intensify feelings of hopelessness or irritability.
4. **Better Focus**
   When well-rested, you can pay attention better. You can handle tasks more easily. Simple things like reading or doing

chores become harder if your mind is foggy from lack of sleep.
5. **Physical Health**
Chronic sleep problems can raise the risk of health issues like heart problems or lowered immunity. A strong body often helps in managing emotional concerns, too. By aiming for better sleep, you support your overall well-being.

Common Sleep Problems During Depression

1. **Trouble Falling Asleep**
Some people lie awake for hours, unable to relax their minds. Worries may race, making it tough to drift off.
2. **Waking Up Often**
Others may fall asleep but wake up multiple times throughout the night. They might have a hard time returning to sleep.
3. **Sleeping Too Much**
Depression can make some people want to stay in bed all day. They might sleep longer than usual and still feel drained.
4. **Light or Unrefreshing Sleep**
You might sleep the right number of hours, but it does not feel restorative. You could toss and turn, or have uneasy dreams.
5. **Nighttime Worries**
Heavy thoughts can pop up just when you try to rest. This can include regret about the past or fear about the future, making relaxation difficult.

Building a Bedtime Routine

1. **Choose a Consistent Bedtime**

- Try to go to bed at the same time each night. This sets your internal clock. Pick a time that allows 7 to 9 hours of sleep if possible.
2. **Wind Down Earlier**
    - About 30 to 60 minutes before bed, do calm activities. Turn off intense shows, put away your phone if you can, and avoid bright lights. This tells your brain it is nearly sleep time.
3. **Gentle Pre-Sleep Habits**
    - Some people find taking a warm shower relaxing. Others like to do light stretches, read a soothing book, or write in a journal to clear the mind. Find a simple routine you can repeat nightly.
4. **Dim the Lights**
    - Harsh or bright lighting can trick your brain into thinking it is still daytime. Use soft lamps or a low light setting to help your body produce sleep-friendly hormones.

Setting Up a Good Sleep Environment

1. **Cool, Dark, and Quiet**
    - Aim for a slightly cool temperature in the bedroom if possible. Use curtains or blinds to block outside light. If noise bothers you, consider earplugs or a gentle sound machine (like soft rain sounds).
2. **Comfortable Bedding**
    - A bed that feels good to you can make a difference. Check if your mattress or pillows are supportive. If you have allergies, wash sheets regularly to keep dust away.
3. **Limit Electronics**
    - TVs, computers, and phones can overstimulate the brain. The light from screens can also keep you awake.

If you must have a phone near you for an alarm, try keeping it face-down or set to "night mode."
4. **Remove Clutter**
    - A messy space can be stressful. If possible, keep your bedroom tidy so it feels more peaceful. You do not need to do a big cleanup all at once; even clearing a small area around your bed can help.

Handling Nighttime Worries

1. **Use a "Worry Notebook"**
    - Keep a small notebook by your bed. If a worry enters your mind, jot it down. This can help you postpone dealing with it until morning. Often, the act of writing it down helps the brain let go.
2. **Reassuring Self-Talk**
    - Gently remind yourself, "I cannot fix everything right now. I will handle it tomorrow when I am rested." This can lower urgency in your thoughts.
3. **Relaxation Techniques**
    - Deep breathing: Inhale for four counts, then exhale for four counts.
    - Muscle relaxation: Tighten and release each muscle group from toes to head.
    - Calming images: Imagine a safe or soothing place, focusing on details like sounds or smells.
4. **Stay Out of Bed If You Cannot Sleep**
    - If you lie awake longer than 20 minutes, get up and do a quiet activity in low light. Maybe read a calming page or do gentle stretches. Return to bed when you feel drowsy. This helps your brain link the bed with sleep, not tossing and turning.

Limiting Sleep Disruptors

1. **Caffeine**
   - Drinking coffee, tea, or soda late in the day can keep you awake. Try to avoid caffeine after lunchtime if you are sensitive.
2. **Heavy Meals or Spicy Foods**
   - Large or spicy dinners might cause heartburn or discomfort, which can disturb sleep. Aim for lighter evening meals or eat earlier to give your body time to digest.
3. **Excessive Screen Time**
   - Spending hours on your phone or computer at night can make the mind too active. If you watch shows in the evening, try stopping at least 30 minutes before bed.
4. **Late-Day Naps**
   - A short nap earlier in the day can be helpful, but long naps close to bedtime can rob you of nighttime rest. Keep naps under 30 minutes if you must nap, and try to do them before mid-afternoon.

Linking Sleep to Daytime Habits

1. **Get Sunshine in the Morning**
   - Exposure to natural light soon after waking helps set your internal clock. Open curtains or step outside for a bit if possible.
2. **Routine Physical Activity**
   - Gentle movement, like walking or light exercise, can help you sleep better at night. Try not to do intense workouts right before bed.
3. **Manage Stress During the Day**
   - If worries pile up all day, they can follow you to bed. Taking short breaks to calm down or talk about problems can lessen nighttime overthinking.

4. **Limit Late-Night Activities**
    - Keep evening tasks low-stress if you can. For example, finishing a big homework assignment or serious work project right before bed can keep your brain buzzing.

When Sleep Feels Impossible

Sometimes, despite your best efforts, sleep does not come. This can happen during high-stress periods or when your sadness is very deep. Here are extra steps to consider:

1. **Check for Underlying Issues**
    - Certain medical conditions, like thyroid problems or sleep disorders, might cause insomnia. If sleep problems persist, speak with a doctor to rule out these issues.
2. **Talk to a Counselor**
    - A mental health professional can teach you more detailed sleep strategies. They might suggest specific relaxation exercises or help you manage deeper causes of your low mood and restlessness.
3. **Consider Medication**
    - Some doctors prescribe short-term sleep aids. If your lack of sleep is severe, ask a professional if medication is an option. Keep in mind that medication alone is not a complete fix. It often works best with better daily habits.
4. **Be Kind to Yourself**
    - Struggling to sleep can be frustrating. Getting angry at yourself for not sleeping might make it even harder to rest. Instead, remind yourself that this is a challenge you are working on, and it will take time.

Handling Oversleeping

1. **Set an Alarm You Can Manage**
   - Sleeping too long might give a temporary escape from sad feelings, but it often leads to feeling groggy and disconnected. Try to wake up at a set time most days, even if it feels tough at first.
2. **Open Curtains**
   - Sunlight can help signal your brain that it is morning. If you tend to oversleep, open your curtains or blinds right after getting up to let light in.
3. **Plan a Morning Task**
   - If you have something small to do in the morning (like a simple chore or a call), you have a reason to get up. Having a little responsibility can push you to leave bed.
4. **Gradual Adjustments**
   - If you are used to waking up at noon, try setting your alarm 15 or 30 minutes earlier each day until you reach a healthier wake-up time. Slow changes can be easier to handle than a sudden shift.

Dreams and Nightmares

1. **Stressful Dreams**
   - Depression and anxiety can lead to vivid or upsetting dreams. You might wake up feeling shaky or upset. Writing these dreams down can help get them out of your head.
2. **Night Terrors**
   - These are intense nightmares that can cause panic. If they happen often, consider talking to a counselor or doctor. Sometimes, lowering stress in daily life can reduce their frequency.

3. **Comforting Yourself After a Bad Dream**
   - If you wake up scared, try deep breathing to steady your heart rate. Remind yourself the dream is over. Sometimes, getting a glass of water or turning on a small light can help you feel safer before going back to bed.
4. **Keeping Track**
   - If your dreams are often disturbing, note how often they happen and what seems to trigger them. This information can be useful when seeking professional advice.

Cultural or Family Sleep Traditions

Different families have different customs around bedtime. Some might pray or share a story together. Others might have a habit like a warm cup of caffeine-free tea. These rituals can bring comfort and signal your mind that it is time to rest. If you like something from your family tradition, keep it. If it does not help, think of trying a new habit. The goal is to create a sense of calm.

Dealing with Shift Work or Unusual Schedules

Not everyone has a traditional 9-to-5 day. If you work at night or have changing shifts, or if your school schedule is unusual, you can still aim for good sleep habits:

1. **Darken Your Room for Daytime Sleep**
   - If you must sleep during the day, use blackout curtains or an eye mask to trick your brain into thinking it is night. Wear earplugs if daytime sounds bother you.
2. **Stay Consistent When Possible**

- Keep the same sleep and wake times on your days off if you can. Switching between day and night sleep constantly can confuse your body clock.
3. **Find Pocket Times to Rest**
   - If your schedule is split, you might get a block of rest in one part of the day and a shorter nap later. Plan these rest periods carefully so you are not going too long without any sleep.
4. **Communicate Your Needs**
   - Let family or roommates know your rest hours so they do not disturb you. Ask them to keep noise low during your main sleep period.

Special Tips for Children and Teens

1. **Bedtime Stories or Relaxing Music**
   - A short, calm story or quiet music can help younger kids unwind. Even teens might like a gentle audio track to focus on as they drift off.
2. **Limited Afternoon Screen Time**
   - Some teens stay up too late on phones or gaming devices, which can throw off natural sleep rhythms. Setting a cutoff an hour before bedtime might help.
3. **Talking About Worries**
   - Younger folks might feel nervous about school or friends. Talking to a parent, older sibling, or trusted adult before bed can help clear out worries so they are not carried into the night.
4. **Consistent Wake-Up for School**
   - Even on weekends, sleeping half the day can make Monday morning harder. Sticking to a reasonably consistent wake-up time helps keep the body clock on track.

Checking for Improvements

1. **Look for Changes in Mood**
   - After a week or two of trying better sleep habits, notice if you feel slightly clearer or calmer. Even small improvements matter.
2. **Note Energy Levels**
   - See if it becomes a bit easier to get through daily tasks or concentrate on reading or schoolwork. This can be a sign your body is resting better.
3. **Track Sleep Patterns**
   - Keep a simple sleep diary: record when you went to bed, when you woke up, and how refreshed you felt. Over time, patterns might emerge that help you fine-tune your approach.

Avoiding Perfection

1. **Occasional Bad Nights Happen**
   - You might do everything right and still have a restless night. That does not mean your efforts are pointless. Give it another try the next night.
2. **Sleep Needs Vary**
   - Some people need 9 hours, while others function well on 7. Listen to your body. Keep aiming for a range of hours that leaves you feeling rested.
3. **No "Perfect" Schedule**
   - Everyone's life is different. You may have responsibilities that shift your bedtime or require early waking. Do the best you can within your circumstances.
4. **Combine Methods**
   - Sleep habits work best when paired with other supportive actions, like stress reduction or good

nutrition. Think of them as pieces of a puzzle that fit together.

Encouraging Yourself

If depression makes it hard to start these changes, remember that better sleep can be a big help in feeling steadier. Even small steps—like turning off screens 15 minutes earlier or trying a simple breathing exercise before bed—can lead to gradual improvements. When you notice a bit more energy in the morning or less trouble falling asleep, that can reinforce the idea that these methods are worth doing.

Moving Ahead

Sleep is a cornerstone of good health, especially when dealing with low mood. By shaping a bedtime routine, creating a calm environment, and easing worries, you can increase your chances of restful nights. This will not solve all problems, but it can make each day a little more manageable. Consistency is key. As you keep up these habits, your body may begin to learn a healthier sleep rhythm, giving you a stronger base to cope with sadness or stress.

In the next chapter, we will talk about easing tension. Everyday worries can tense up the body and mind, making sleep and daily life more difficult. Learning ways to reduce tension can improve how you feel physically and emotionally. By combining better sleep with methods to calm tension, you can help yourself gain a more balanced mood.

Chapter 12: Easing Tension

Tension can build in your muscles, thoughts, and emotions. When you are feeling low, you might notice your shoulders creeping up, your jaw clenched, or your stomach in knots. This physical tightness can feed into mental stress, creating a loop that makes it harder to relax or handle problems. In this chapter, we will look at what tension is, how it shows up, and ways to ease it. By learning these strategies, you can help your body let go, which can bring a sense of relief and even lighten your mood.

What Is Tension?

1. **Physical Tightness**
   Tension often shows up as stiffness in areas like the neck, shoulders, or back. You might feel knots in your muscles or notice that you are grinding your teeth without realizing it.
2. **Emotional Strain**
   When you are upset or worried, your body reflects that. Emotions and stress can lead to clenched fists, shallow breathing, or an uneasy stomach.
3. **Mental Pressure**
   Your mind can feel overloaded. Negative thoughts or worry can make it tough to concentrate on tasks. This mental load can keep the body in a state of high alert, leading to more tension.
4. **Link to Stress Response**
   When facing a threat, your body goes into "fight or flight" mode. Muscles tighten, heart rate speeds up, and you get ready to act. But if stress is constant—even daily concerns—your body might stay partially stuck in that mode, creating ongoing tension.

Signs You Are Tense

1. **Aching Muscles**
   Soreness or pain in the neck, shoulders, or lower back that does not come from exercise can be a clue that tension has built up.
2. **Frequent Headaches**
   Tension in the scalp, jaw, or neck can trigger headaches. Some people get headaches across the forehead or at the back of the head.
3. **Shallow Breathing**
   When stressed, you might breathe with quick, small breaths, mainly in your chest rather than deeply into your belly.
4. **Difficulty Relaxing**
   You may feel on edge, unable to sit still or calm your thoughts. Restless legs or tapping fingers can indicate stored-up energy.
5. **Irritability**
   Tension can affect mood. If you find yourself snapping at small things, it could be because your body and mind are stretched thin.

Why Tension Can Worsen Sadness

1. **Ongoing Stress**
   Living with a tight, tense body can keep stress hormones higher. This constant state of alert can deepen feelings of sadness or anxiety.
2. **Reduced Comfort**
   Physical pain or stiffness can add to mental burdens. It is harder to handle emotions gracefully when your back hurts or your neck is stiff.

3. **Less Energy**
   Being tense all the time can be draining. You spend more energy just holding your muscles in a rigid state, leaving you feeling fatigued.
4. **Poor Rest**
   Tension often carries over into nighttime, making it tough to wind down for sleep. As discussed in the previous chapter, poor rest can fuel depression.

Strategies to Ease Tension

1. **Progressive Muscle Relaxation (PMR)**
   - **How**: Start at your toes. Tighten your foot muscles for a few seconds, then release. Move up to your calves, thighs, belly, hands, arms, shoulders, and so on.
   - **Why**: By tensing then releasing, you teach your muscles what true relaxation feels like. PMR can also distract your mind from negative thoughts.
2. **Gentle Stretching**
   - **Why**: Slow stretches increase blood flow and loosen tight areas.
   - **How**: Pick simple stretches like rolling your shoulders backward and forward, reaching your arms overhead, or gently twisting your upper body side to side. Move slowly to avoid injury.
3. **Mindful Breathing**
   - **How**: Sit or stand comfortably. Inhale slowly, letting your belly expand. Exhale fully, feeling your body soften.
   - **When**: You can do this anytime—while waiting in line, sitting at your desk, or lying in bed. It can be especially helpful when you first notice tension building.
4. **Warm Shower or Bath**

- **Benefit**: Warm water can relax tight muscles. Some people find adding calming scents (like lavender) helps them feel even more at ease.
- **Caution**: Make sure the temperature is not too hot, and keep the bathroom safe to prevent slips.

5. **Massage or Self-Massage**
    - **Option**: If you have access, a professional massage can be very soothing. But self-massage can help too. Gently press or rub areas like the neck or shoulders in small circles.
    - **Effect**: This can release knots and remind you to unclench tense spots.

Quick Tension-Relief Exercises

1. **Shoulder Shrug and Drop**
    - **Method**: Lift your shoulders up to your ears. Hold for a count of three, then drop them down. Repeat a few times.
    - **Result**: Helps release built-up stress in the neck and shoulder region.
2. **Jaw Release**
    - **Method**: Open your mouth wide for a moment, then let it close gently. Move your lower jaw side to side.
    - **Result**: Reduces tightness from teeth clenching or grinding.
3. **Shake It Out**
    - **Method**: Gently shake your hands, arms, or even your legs. Picture the tension leaving your body as you do it.
    - **Result**: Loosens stiff muscles and can also be a quick burst of playful movement.
4. **Forehead Smoothing**

- **Method**: Lightly run your fingertips across your forehead from the center out to the sides. This can also be done on the scalp.
- **Result**: Helps release tension that can lead to headaches.

Longer Relaxation Methods

1. **Yoga or Tai Chi**
   - **Why**: These practices combine slow movement with mindful breathing. They can strengthen your body gently while teaching you to be aware of tension.
   - **How**: Look for beginner-friendly videos or classes. The movements do not have to be complicated to be effective.
2. **Meditation**
   - **Basics**: Sit quietly and focus on your breathing or repeat a calming phrase in your mind. If your thoughts wander, gently bring them back.
   - **Benefit**: Over time, meditation can help you notice tension early and let it go before it piles up.
3. **Guided Relaxation Recordings**
   - **Option**: Many free apps and online resources offer guided steps to relax your body and mind.
   - **Process**: Follow the voice instructions, which might guide you through muscle relaxation, calming images, or gentle breathing.
4. **Nature Walk**
   - **Why**: Spending time in a park or near trees can help slow racing thoughts and relax the body. Breathing fresh air can also ease physical tension.
   - **How**: Walk at a comfortable pace, noticing sights and sounds around you. Focus on each step instead of worries.

Handling Sudden Tension in Stressful Moments

1. **Pause and Breathe**
    - When something triggers you—like an argument or a piece of bad news—pause if you can. Take one or two slow, deep breaths. This can prevent tension from escalating.
2. **Grounding Techniques**
    - Look around and name five things you see, four things you can touch, three things you can hear, two things you can smell, and one thing you can taste (if applicable). This shifts your attention away from tension and back to the present.
3. **Move Away Briefly**
    - If possible, step outside or into another room for a moment. Changing your location can interrupt the stress loop, giving you a chance to calm your body.
4. **Soothe with Touch**
    - Gently rub your arms or place a hand over your heart. Sometimes, a simple physical gesture can remind you to soften and breathe.

Linking Tension Release to Your Daily Routine

1. **Morning Stretch**
    - Start your day with gentle stretches to wake up your muscles. This can keep tension from building later.
2. **Mini-Breaks**
    - If you have a desk job or long classes, take a minute or two every hour to stretch or do quick breathing. This prevents tension from piling up over the day.
3. **Pre-Bed Unwind**

- Spend a few minutes stretching or doing a slow routine before bed. This can help release the day's stress so you sleep more easily.
4. **Pair Tension Relief with Other Tasks**
    - If you are waiting for something (like the microwave timer), use that time for a brief shoulder roll or deep breath. Make tension relief part of everyday moments.

When Tension Feels Overwhelming

1. **Check for Medical Causes**
    - Sometimes, intense muscle pain or persistent tension might have a physical reason, such as a pulled muscle or an underlying medical issue. A doctor can help rule these out.
2. **Talk to a Professional**
    - If tension links to severe anxiety or past trauma, a counselor can give specialized techniques. They might teach you more focused stress-management exercises.
3. **Physical Therapy**
    - If your tension causes ongoing pain or posture problems, a physical therapist can guide you with targeted stretches and exercises.
4. **Supportive Help**
    - If daily tasks are too difficult because of tension or low mood, ask a friend or family member to lend a hand. Reducing some burdens can help you focus on relaxation.

Using Tools and Aids

1. **Heat Packs or Warm Compresses**
   - Applying gentle warmth to a tight area (like the neck) can loosen muscles. Just follow safety guidelines to avoid burning your skin.
2. **Relaxation Apps**
   - Some apps offer quick sessions that guide you to relax certain muscle groups or slow your breathing.
3. **Foam Rollers or Massage Balls**
   - These items help you apply pressure to tense spots, especially in the back or legs. Start slowly and do not press too hard.
4. **Aromatherapy (If You Like It)**
   - Soft scents like lavender or chamomile in a diffuser or lotion can soothe some people. Make sure you are not allergic or sensitive to the smell.

Lifestyle Factors That Lower Tension

1. **Steady Movement**
   - Regular walks or gentle exercise can help manage overall stress and loosen tight muscles over time.
2. **Balanced Diet**
   - Eating balanced meals can keep your energy stable. Lack of proper nutrition can leave you feeling weaker and more prone to stress reactions.
3. **Hydration**
   - Drink enough water. Dehydration can worsen headaches and muscle cramps, adding another layer of discomfort.
4. **Social Support**

- Talking with friends or loved ones about problems can ease mental pressure. Feeling understood often helps the body loosen up.

Tension and Anger

1. **Connection**
   - Anger and tension can fuel each other. If you feel tense, small things might irritate you more. If you get angry, your muscles might clench further.
2. **Cooling Down**
   - In a moment of anger, try the shoulder drop or deep breathing. Remind yourself to unclench your fists or release your jaw.
3. **Using Healthy Outlets**
   - Express anger in ways that do not harm you or others—such as scribbling on paper, talking to a trusted friend, or writing in a journal.
4. **Learning Triggers**
   - Pay attention to the people or situations that spark tension and anger. Over time, you can plan ways to respond differently or limit contact if possible.

Combining Tension Relief with Emotional Support

1. **Talk Therapy**
   - Some tension stems from unresolved issues. A mental health professional can help you process feelings and reduce stress responses.
2. **Support Groups**

- Joining a group (in person or online) where people discuss similar challenges can help you see you are not alone. This sense of connection can lower tension.
3. **Hobbies and Activities**
    - Doing something you find calming—like drawing, gardening, or light sports—can let your mind and body relax. Engaging in a pleasant task takes the focus off worries.
4. **Spiritual or Reflective Practices**
    - Some people find relief in prayer, reflective reading, or quiet time in a peaceful setting. This can create a sense of calm that carries over into physical ease.

Noticing When Tension Returns

1. **Body Scan**
    - Once or twice a day, pause and mentally scan your body from head to toe. If you find tight spots (like shoulders or jaw), do a quick release method.
2. **Short Journal Notes**
    - You could jot down when you feel a sudden spike in tension. Note what happened right before it. Over time, you might spot patterns and learn to prevent or handle those triggers.
3. **Ask for Feedback**
    - Sometimes, friends or family notice signs of tension before you do. If they say, "You seem stiff," take a moment to breathe and loosen up.
4. **Plan Ahead**
    - If you know a stressful event is coming (like a test or a difficult conversation), schedule time to do a short tension-relief exercise both before and after.

Gently Encouraging Yourself

1. **Patience**
   - It might take a while to fully relax. Tension can be a long-term habit, especially if sadness has been present for a while. Stick with the methods you find helpful.
2. **Kind Words to Yourself**
   - You could say, "My body is trying to protect me by tightening up, but I can gently let go." Simple phrases like this can replace harsh self-criticism.
3. **Combine Tactics**
   - For stubborn tension, layer multiple methods: try a warm shower, then do a short breathing exercise, followed by gentle stretching. Stacking calm actions can multiply the effect.

Future Benefits of Less Tension

1. **Increased Comfort**
   - Reducing tension means fewer aches and less physical stress. This can help you feel lighter overall.
2. **Better Sleep**
   - Relaxed muscles and a calmer mind often lead to better rest. As we talked about in the last chapter, sleeping well can help reduce sadness.
3. **Clearer Thinking**
   - When tension is low, your mind can focus on tasks and problem-solving instead of managing pain or tightness.
4. **Healthier Mood**
   - Low tension can mean lower stress hormones, which might help lift your overall mood bit by bit.

Putting It All into Practice

Tension relief does not have to be complicated. Start with a simple exercise—maybe a shoulder roll or a breathing pause—and try it once a day. Notice how your body feels. Gradually add more methods if you want. Over time, as your body learns to relax more often, you might see an improvement in how you handle everyday stresses.

If you find tension is deeply rooted or tied to serious trauma or anxiety, seeking professional guidance can be an important step. They can show you advanced techniques or point you toward programs that help people with similar struggles. Remember that tension release is just one piece of the bigger puzzle of managing sadness. It works well alongside healthy sleep, supportive relationships, and managing negative thoughts.

Moving Forward

Learning to ease tension gives you a powerful tool against daily stress and low mood. By loosening tight muscles and calming your mind, you create a safer internal space for yourself. This can open the door to seeing more clearly, making better decisions, and feeling a little bit stronger. In the chapters ahead, we will talk about more creative ways to handle feelings, including arts and expression. Combining tension release methods with expressive outlets can deepen the sense of relief and help you find moments of peace.

Just remember: tension tends to return if daily stress stays high. Keep practicing these tips as part of your routine, adjusting them when life changes. Over time, your body might learn to recognize tension early and let go, helping you find a greater sense of ease each day.

Chapter 13: Arts and Expression

Arts and creative expression can offer a refreshing way to handle low mood. When you feel sad or worried, it might help to paint, draw, write poems, or even dance. These activities let you express what you are feeling inside without needing perfect words or lengthy explanations. You do not need to be a skilled artist for creative activities to help. The simple act of making something can bring a bit of relief and remind you that there are still sparks of color and brightness in life. In this chapter, we will explore how various forms of art—such as drawing, writing, music, crafts, and more—can support better emotional health. You will find ideas to try, ways to keep going if you feel discouraged, and tips to stay motivated even when sadness is strong.

Why Creativity Supports Emotional Health

1. **Outlet for Feelings**
   Some experiences are hard to capture in everyday speech. Art provides other ways to show how you feel. Perhaps you do not want to talk about your sadness, but painting swirls of dark or bright color might reveal the same emotion. In this sense, creativity offers a release.
2. **Lower Stress**
   Engaging in art can calm your mind. When you focus on shapes, colors, words, or notes, your thoughts about worry or sadness can soften. Even a short session can lower stress hormones and slow a racing mind.
3. **A Sense of Control**
   When depressed, you may feel you have no power over your own thoughts or events around you. Making art—even something small—can remind you that you can shape something. This can spark a gentle feeling of capability.

4. **Connection with Others**
   Sharing art, poems, or songs with people you trust can be a way to bridge lonely feelings. Sometimes, others see your work and relate to it, realizing they are not alone. This can create safe and supportive interactions.
5. **Moments of Pleasure or Curiosity**
   Depression often steals pleasure. Creative tasks can deliver small sparks of interest, letting you become curious about how colors mix or how words form a poem. These moments of curiosity can be small steps toward feeling better.

Types of Artistic Expression

1. **Drawing and Painting**
   - **How to Start**: You do not need fancy tools. A regular pencil and paper are enough. If you want color, crayons or inexpensive paints can be used.
   - **Why It Helps**: The process of moving the pencil or brush can focus your mind on the present moment. You might explore using light or dark shades to reflect your mood.
2. **Collage**
   - **How to Start**: Gather old magazines, newspapers, or scraps. Cut or tear out pictures and words that catch your attention. Glue them onto paper in a way that feels meaningful.
   - **Why It Helps**: Collage is a flexible art form. You do not have to draw. You pick images or words that speak to your emotions, forming a visual story.
3. **Sculpting or Clay Work**
   - **How to Start**: Many craft stores sell air-dry clay. You can shape it by hand, then let it harden. If you do not have clay, you can try homemade dough using flour, water, and salt.

- **Why It Helps**: Handling clay can be soothing. The feeling of the material in your hands can help channel restlessness or worry into a creative act. You do not need skill—just squeeze, shape, or roll as you wish.

4. **Music or Singing**
    - **How to Start**: Hum your favorite tune, sing softly in your room, or try a simple instrument if you have one. Even drumming lightly on a table can be a form of expression.
    - **Why It Helps**: Music affects our emotions directly. Singing or playing even a single note rhythmically can shift your mood a bit or release stored-up tension.

5. **Writing Poems or Stories**
    - **How to Start**: Pick a small notebook or open a blank document. Jot down lines that describe your day, your hopes, or even the color of your sadness. You could write a short story or a few lines that rhyme.
    - **Why It Helps**: Putting thoughts into words—even if they are jumbled—can bring some structure to messy feelings. Poems let you be symbolic without strict rules.

6. **Dance or Movement**
    - **How to Start**: Find a private space, put on music you like, and move around in a way that feels natural. It does not have to be a formal dance. Even gentle swaying is fine.
    - **Why It Helps**: Moving your body can loosen tension and allow energy to flow. This can bring a hint of relief or release pent-up emotions, especially if you have been feeling stiff or agitated.

7. **Photography**
    - **How to Start**: Use a phone camera or any basic camera to capture images that stand out to you—light and shadow, objects in your home, or interesting views outside.

- **Why It Helps**: Looking through a camera lens encourages you to notice details you might otherwise overlook. This shift in focus can calm anxious thoughts.

Overcoming Common Blocks

1. **"I'm Not an Artist"**
    - It is easy to think you have no talent if you do not draw or write well. However, creative expression is not about being perfect. Childlike scribbles, abstract shapes, or short rhymes can still help you express yourself.
2. **Fear of Judgment**
    - You might worry that others will see your art and judge it. If so, keep your work private at first. You only need to share it when you feel ready or if you think it might help you connect with someone safe.
3. **Lack of Motivation**
    - Depression can sap your energy. Start small. Sketch for five minutes. Write a few words. Hum a tune for 30 seconds. These tiny steps can still help lift your mood even if you do not produce a big project.
4. **Time Constraints**
    - You do not need hours. A brief break to doodle or jot down lines in a notebook can be enough. Fit creativity into small pockets of your day—like during a quiet moment before bed.
5. **Feeling Overwhelmed**
    - If you feel swamped, pick a simple, low-pressure activity. For instance, just color in a coloring sheet or draw shapes. Let the activity soothe you instead of becoming another chore.

Turning Feelings into Art

1. **Color and Emotion**
   - Each color can represent a mood. Red might show anger or energy, blue might reflect sadness or calm, yellow might hint at hope or slight brightness. You can pick colors that match what you feel or try opposite ones to see if that shifts your mood.
2. **Lines and Shapes**
   - Smooth lines might show peace, while jagged lines could reveal tension. Circles can show wholeness, and scattered dots might represent confusion. There are no limits. Let your hand move freely.
3. **Symbols**
   - You might draw or craft symbols of how you feel, such as a broken heart to show hurt, a small flame for hope, or a wilted flower for exhaustion. Turning an abstract feeling into a symbol can clarify what is going on inside.
4. **Music Choices**
   - If you are feeling agitated, you might pick slower or softer music to ease that feeling. If you are feeling numb, a more upbeat tune could stir some energy. Singing or humming along can further link your emotions to the sound.

Using Art to Spot Changes in Mood

1. **Visual Diary**
   - Keep a sketchbook where each day you draw or paint a page that shows how you feel. Over time, you can look back and see patterns. Maybe you notice more bright colors on certain days, or swirling lines when you are anxious.

2. **Writing Log**
   - A few lines of written reflection each day can track your emotional ups and downs. Even if you just scribble words like "tired," "hopeful," or "worried," you have a record of shifts. This can help you see slow improvements over weeks or months.
3. **Playlist Shifts**
   - Notice which songs or styles you gravitate to during low periods. You might find that certain songs soothe you or that you use music as a safe outlet for tears or anger. Over time, you may see changes in your choices as your mood improves.
4. **Craft Projects**
   - If you enjoy making things like bracelets or small sculptures, you can note which colors or designs you choose on different days. This can serve as an indirect reflection of your internal state.

Bringing Others into Your Creative Space

1. **Art Partners**
   - Invite a friend or family member to draw or do crafts together. You do not have to talk about your feelings if you do not want to, but simply creating side by side can lessen loneliness.
2. **Group Workshops**
   - Some community centers or libraries offer free art, writing, or music sessions. This can be a way to meet people who share an interest. Just be sure to pick a group that feels comfortable for you.
3. **Online Communities**
   - If you prefer not to attend events in person, you can join online art groups or writing forums. Sharing your work anonymously might give you the reassurance

that people can appreciate your expressions without judging your entire life.
4. **Family Projects**
    - If you live with relatives, propose a simple craft night or a puzzle session. The goal is not to produce perfect art, but to spend relaxed time together. Laughter and casual conversation can arise naturally during these sessions.

Expressing Hard Feelings Safely

1. **Anger or Frustration**
    - Try scribbling aggressively on paper or ripping up scraps to create a collage of rough shapes. Or choose fast, loud music and stomp or dance around (in a safe space). Release built-up energy in ways that do not harm yourself or others.
2. **Deep Sadness**
    - Soft or slower forms of art might help here. Coloring repetitive patterns, like mandalas or simple geometric shapes, can feel soothing. Writing a poem about your sadness can free some of it.
3. **Fear or Anxiety**
    - Quick doodles of what scares you can sometimes make those fears less powerful. Another idea is to craft a small symbol of protection—like a clay charm or a drawn emblem—that you keep as a reminder that you are seeking safety.
4. **Guilt or Shame**
    - Write a letter to yourself (that you do not have to send to anyone). In this letter, let yourself admit what you feel guilty about. Then write some words of understanding or forgiveness. You can keep this letter or tear it up—whatever feels right.

Staying Motivated with Art

1. **Schedule Short Sessions**
   - It might help to plan a quick 10-minute art break a few times a week. Setting aside time reminds you to keep engaging, even when you feel blah or unmotivated.
2. **Keep Supplies Handy**
   - Keep pencils, crayons, or notebooks in easily reachable places. This lowers the barrier to starting a small activity. If you have to dig out materials from a hidden spot, you might lose the will to begin.
3. **Try New Forms**
   - If painting gets dull, switch to photography. If writing feels stale, experiment with making up a quick tune. Changing forms can keep creativity fresh, especially if you are easily bored or discouraged.
4. **Reflect on the Outcome**
   - After you finish a small piece, take a moment to see how you feel. Sometimes, you might feel a small release of tension or a tiny lift in mood. Noticing this result can motivate you to continue later.

What If Art Triggers Sadness?

1. **Understand Triggers**
   - Sometimes, creating can bring up memories or strong emotions. If this happens, pause and breathe. Remind yourself that it is normal to feel deep emotions when you let them out through art.
2. **Take Breaks**
   - If you start feeling overwhelmed, stop the activity. Get a drink of water, step outside, or do a gentle physical movement. You can return to the art when you feel calmer.

3. **Seek Support**
    - If creative expression stirs up very painful thoughts, you might want to talk with a counselor, a trusted friend, or a mental health helpline. Professional help can guide you through these deeper layers safely.
4. **Shift to Something Lighter**
    - If a particular piece feels too heavy, switch to a simpler or more neutral activity. For example, draw a favorite object or focus on doodling patterns rather than exploring intense feelings.

Combining Art with Other Methods

1. **Calming Techniques**
    - Before you start creating, do a quick breathing exercise to get centered (see Chapter 8 on quieting the mind). This can help you feel more present as you express yourself.
2. **Task Planning**
    - If you want to finish a bigger project (like a short story or a painting), break it into smaller steps (see Chapter 10 on planning tasks). This reduces overwhelm.
3. **Physical Activity**
    - After dancing or taking a short walk (see Chapter 7 on staying active), you might find it easier to settle into a creative flow. Movement can clear mental cobwebs.
4. **Supportive Relationships**
    - Showing a friend or counselor something you created can lead to helpful talks about your feelings (see Chapter 4 on building connections). You do not have to share everything, but sometimes an outside viewpoint is reassuring.

Real-Life Example

Imagine a student named Grace who feels down most days. She loves looking at art but always says, "I cannot draw." One afternoon, she decides to try anyway. She uses a pencil to sketch random shapes, circles within circles. She notices it calms her. The next day, she colors them with markers. After about a week of doing this for a few minutes each day, she has a small collection of bright designs. She shows them to her sibling, who says they look interesting. Grace feels a slight sense of pride and keeps going. Over time, these small acts of creativity become a routine that offers her a break from harsh thoughts. She still has sad days, but she knows she can spend 10 or 15 minutes drawing to breathe a bit easier.

Sharing Your Work with Care

1. **Choose Safe People**
   - If you decide to show your art or writing, pick people who tend to be kind or open-minded. Sharing with the wrong person can lead to hurtful comments or misunderstandings.
2. **Set Boundaries**
   - You can say, "I'd like you to see this, but I'm not ready for detailed feedback." Or, "This is personal, so please keep it private." Clear expectations help prevent unwanted judgments or broken trust.
3. **Online Caution**
   - If you post work on social media, remember that comments can be unpredictable. You might want to share in a private group or with a limited set of followers until you feel more comfortable.
4. **Gaining Encouragement**

- Supportive feedback from friends can uplift you. If they enjoy your poem or painting, it can be a small reminder that you have something valuable to express.

Creating a Personal Arts Practice

1. **Set an Intention**
    - Each time you create, decide if you want to explore a specific feeling or just relax. This gentle focus can guide your session.
2. **Gather Materials**
    - Keep it simple. A pencil, a sheet of paper, or a basic music app can be enough to start. Over time, you might add paints, clay, or other items if you wish.
3. **Find Your Time**
    - Whether in the morning, after school or work, or before bed, pick a time that fits your life. Regular practice can help you see more benefits.
4. **End with a Moment of Reflection**
    - After creating, pause. Notice if you feel calmer, lighter, or even more emotional. If you feel heavier, do a quick grounding activity or talk to someone supportive.

Benefits Over Time

1. **Better Self-Awareness**
    - Repeated creative work can help you spot your feelings more clearly. You might see that you often use angry lines on weeks you feel stressed, or that you reach for bright colors when you have bits of hope.
2. **Confidence**

- Making something—no matter how simple—can boost your sense of being able to do things. This can gently counter the negative belief that you cannot accomplish anything.
3. **Healthy Distraction**
    - During tough moments, having a go-to art activity can prevent you from sinking deeper into sad thoughts. It is a healthier form of escape that also allows for expression.
4. **Possibility of Joy**
    - Over time, you might find pockets of pleasure or fascination in your art. Even if sadness remains, these sparks remind you that joy can still exist.

Final Thoughts on Arts and Expression

Art can be your private space or something you share with a small circle. You do not need advanced training or expensive supplies. What matters is the feeling you tap into when you create. Let your art reflect whatever is inside—whether calm, chaos, or both. Over days and weeks, engaging with these small creative acts can bring relief, encourage self-discovery, and offer moments of rest from constant worry.

Chapter 14: Seeing Yourself Kindly

When deep sadness sets in, it can twist how you see yourself. You might think you are worthless, a burden, or undeserving of care. These harsh ideas can become a habit, making it tough to believe good things about who you are. This chapter focuses on learning to view yourself with kindness and understanding. Seeing yourself kindly does not mean ignoring mistakes or pretending life is all good. It means recognizing you are human, with strengths and struggles, worthy of support and empathy. We will discuss what self-kindness looks like, why it matters for those facing depression, and practical ways to begin shifting your inner voice from cruel to caring.

Why Self-Kindness Is Important

1. **Counters Negative Thoughts**
   Depression often brings harsh inner talk. Kindness toward yourself can act as a shield against these self-critical thoughts. When you speak to yourself with warmth, it is harder for shame or guilt to grow.
2. **Reduces Shame**
   Shame can make you hide problems or blame yourself for things outside your control. Self-kindness helps you see mistakes or troubles in a balanced way, without burying yourself in blame.
3. **Supports Emotional Healing**
   Just as a friend's gentle words can help you feel better when you are sad, kind words from yourself can also soothe hurt feelings. This is especially useful when you face disappointments or triggers in daily life.
4. **Encourages Positive Choices**
   When you like and respect yourself, you are more likely to treat your body and mind well. You might take steps to eat

better, get rest, or reach out for help. Self-kindness can be a motivator for healthier actions.

Common Barriers to Self-Kindness

1. **Harsh Upbringing**
   If you grew up in an environment where caregivers or peers regularly criticized you, you might have learned to speak to yourself in the same harsh tone.
2. **Perfectionism**
   Thinking everything must be flawless can lead to big self-criticism when you fall short. You may find it hard to be gentle with yourself because you feel like you must be perfect.
3. **Fear of Being "Selfish"**
   Some worry that being kind to themselves is indulgent or wrong. In reality, caring for yourself is not selfish. It gives you a stronger base to contribute to the world and help others.
4. **Mixing Self-Worth with Productivity**
   Many people believe they are only valuable if they constantly achieve. When depression reduces your energy or success at tasks, you might feel worthless. Learning self-kindness means separating your innate worth from what you accomplish.

Small Shifts Toward a Kinder View

1. **Use Gentler Language**
   - Instead of "I failed that test because I am stupid," say, "That test was tough. I did my best, and I can improve next time."
   - Notice that you are not ignoring the issue (doing poorly on a test) but are removing the insulting label about yourself.

2. **Recall a Supportive Voice**
   - Think of someone who has shown you genuine care—a teacher, friend, or relative. Imagine how they might comfort you if you spoke harshly about yourself. Try adopting that warmer tone in your own thoughts.
3. **Write Down Positive Comments**
   - If someone says something nice about you, jot it down. Keep a small list of good feedback. When depression hits, reading those comments can remind you that you have qualities others appreciate.
4. **Talk to Yourself as a Friend**
   - If you would not say something mean to a close friend who is struggling, do not say it to yourself. This comparison often reveals how unkind we can be to our own minds.

Handling Self-Blame

1. **List Factors**
   - When you blame yourself for a negative outcome, list out other causes. For example, if you did poorly on a project, was there limited time, unclear instructions, or outside stress? Recognizing multiple factors can soften total self-blame.
2. **Learn from Mistakes**
   - Instead of focusing on the shame of a mistake, ask, "What can I learn from this?" This shifts the focus to growth rather than punishment. Even a small insight can lead to self-improvement without harshness.
3. **Set Realistic Standards**
   - If you find that your expectations are unreasonably high, adjust them. This does not mean settling for poor effort; it means being fair about what is possible given your resources, time, and emotional state.

4. **Seek Understanding, Not Punishment**
    - When you feel you have done something wrong, consider gentle apologies or actions to correct it. Punishing yourself with unkind thoughts rarely fixes the problem—it just amplifies sadness.

Practical Exercises for Self-Kindness

1. **Mirror Affirmations**
    - Stand or sit in front of a mirror. Say simple, truthful statements like, "I am doing my best today," or "I deserve understanding." It can feel strange at first, but repeating kind words can begin to chip away at negative self-image.
2. **Self-Kindness Notes**
    - Place small sticky notes around your living space with gentle reminders: "Remember, be patient with yourself," or "You matter." Reading them daily can reduce the automatic nature of self-criticism.
3. **Compassionate Letter**
    - Write a letter to yourself describing your struggles. Then respond with the same kindness you would offer a dear friend. Include phrases of support and understanding. Keep it somewhere safe to reread when needed.
4. **Body Kindness Ritual**
    - Gently touch your arm or hug yourself and say something like, "I am here for you." This might sound odd, but simple physical gestures can create a feeling of warmth toward yourself.

Changing Self-Talk in Daily Situations

1. **Morning Wake-Up**
   - If you wake up dreading the day, shift the thought from "I can't handle this" to "I'll take things step by step." Acknowledge that facing the day can be tough, but you can tackle it in smaller parts.
2. **Handling Mistakes**
   - When a mistake happens, move from "I am terrible" to "I made an error, but I can still fix things or learn for next time." Let the moment pass without letting it define your entire self-worth.
3. **Receiving Criticism**
   - If someone criticizes you, pause before you turn that into self-hate. Ask if the criticism is fair or if it reflects their own perspective. Then consider how to respond in a balanced way, without calling yourself names.
4. **Evening Reflection**
   - Before bed, note one thing you handled okay that day. It does not have to be huge—maybe you took a short walk or finished a minor task. Reminding yourself of even small positives can lessen the weight of negative thoughts.

The Role of Forgiveness

1. **Forgiving Yourself for Past Mistakes**
   - Everyone makes errors. If you hold onto guilt, it can keep you stuck. Think about what steps you can take today to be kinder to yourself about things you did not do perfectly in the past.
2. **Understanding "I Did Then What I Knew"**
   - Often, we do the best we can with the information and emotional state we had at the time. Recognizing this

might help you let go of harsh judgments that do not match your current knowledge or maturity.
3. **Balancing Accountability and Kindness**
    - Self-forgiveness does not mean ignoring harmful actions. If you need to apologize or change a behavior, do so. But do not condemn your entire character forever—learning and growing is part of being human.
4. **Seeking Support from a Counselor**
    - If self-forgiveness is very hard, a counselor can guide you through deeper healing steps, possibly using methods tailored to your situation. They can help you safely address any guilt or shame.

Seeing Strengths Alongside Weaknesses

1. **Write a Balanced List**
    - List a few qualities you like about yourself, and also list areas you want to improve. Having both on the same page shows that nobody is just strengths or just weaknesses.
2. **Appreciate Small Wins**
    - If you find cooking a simple meal hard, but you managed to do it, recognize that. You might think it is small, but acknowledging small efforts can build a kinder outlook on what you can do.
3. **Practice Accepting Praise**
    - When someone gives a compliment, you might feel tempted to reject it. Try responding with "Thank you" instead of brushing it off. This small act can open you up to letting kindness in from others.
4. **Recognize Shared Humanity**
    - Remember that nobody is perfect or problem-free. Feeling sad or making mistakes is part of being human. Seeing this truth can ease the sting of self-criticism.

Handling Doubts About Self-Kindness

1. **"I Don't Deserve It"**
   - Depression might tell you that you do not deserve any kindness. However, this thought is a symptom of the condition. Every person deserves basic compassion, including you.
2. **"This Won't Change Anything"**
   - At first, it might seem like a few kinder words cannot fight heavy sadness. But repeated acts of self-kindness can gradually reshape how you relate to yourself, improving your ability to manage problems.
3. **"I'm Too Used to Being Harsh"**
   - Longstanding habits can be hard to break. You can start by noticing each harsh thought and, right after, adding a gentle correction. Over time, the new habit can form, even if it feels forced at first.
4. **"Others Have It Worse"**
   - You may think you are not allowed to be kind to yourself because other people suffer more. Pain is not a contest. You can acknowledge others' struggles while also allowing yourself kindness.

Supporting Self-Kindness with Daily Habits

1. **Healthy Routines**
   - Things like regular sleep, balanced meals, and planned tasks (covered in earlier chapters) show you care about yourself enough to meet your basic needs. This is an indirect form of self-kindness.
2. **Peaceful Pastimes**
   - Enjoying gentle activities like reading, music, or calm hobbies can remind you that you are worthy of

moments of rest and pleasure. This helps combat negative self-beliefs.
3. **Physical Care**
   - Whether taking a warm bath, doing light stretches, or taking a short walk, treating your body well can reinforce self-kindness. You learn to respect and nourish yourself instead of ignoring or punishing your body.
4. **Connecting with Supporters**
   - Spending time with friends, mentors, or caring family members can reinforce the idea that you are not alone. Their kindness can mirror the kindness you want to grow toward yourself.

Watching Out for Self-Kindness Pitfalls

1. **Ignoring Real Problems**
   - Being kind to yourself does not mean avoiding responsibilities. If an issue needs attention, address it with a caring mindset, rather than pushing it away.
2. **Slipping into Self-Pity**
   - Kindness is not about feeling sorry for yourself forever. It is about gentle understanding. Self-pity can trap you in a feeling of hopelessness. Self-kindness focuses on seeing your hurt and also believing you can heal or improve.
3. **Waiting for Others to Approve**
   - Self-kindness is something you can practice regardless of how others treat you. Although it is nice when people support your kinder self-view, do not depend on external praise to keep it going.
4. **Forgetting Boundaries**

- Being kind to yourself also means setting limits. If someone is draining you or treating you badly, self-kindness might mean stepping away or saying no.

Checking Your Progress

1. **Notice Less Harsh Self-Talk**
   - After some time, you might catch fewer extreme statements like, "I'm a total failure." You might switch to, "I'm upset with how that went, but I can try again."
2. **Feelings of Relief**
   - Self-kindness can bring small waves of relief or lightness, even in the middle of difficulties. You might sense a gentler tone in your mind, which can reduce tension.
3. **Improved Mood Over Time**
   - Although it might not be a sudden leap, day-by-day kindness can chip away at deep sadness. You may have slightly more neutral or positive moments in your emotional landscape.
4. **Willingness to Try**
   - People who are kinder to themselves often attempt new coping methods or make more effort in daily tasks. Self-kindness fosters hope, which can spark fresh attempts at dealing with problems.

Real-Life Example

Consider Daniel, who often calls himself "useless" if he does not achieve perfection in school. He starts practicing self-kindness by noticing each time he says "I'm so dumb." Whenever he catches that phrase, he gently replaces it with, "I'm feeling frustrated because that was hard. I'm not dumb; I just need more practice." It feels forced at first, but over weeks of doing this, Daniel notices he feels less ashamed about asking for help. He reaches out to a tutor and improves bit by bit. The shift did not happen overnight, but his new inner voice helped him keep trying.

Pairing Self-Kindness with Other Supports

1. **Therapy**
    - A counselor can help you work through deeper negative beliefs. They might show you exercises tailored to your thinking patterns, strengthening your self-kindness practice.
2. **Medication**
    - If a doctor prescribes medication for depression, improved mood balance can make it easier to adopt a kinder internal voice. You can practice self-kindness more effectively when extreme sadness is managed.
3. **Creative Expression**
    - As covered in Chapter 13, art or writing can let you show compassion toward yourself in a symbolic way. You might draw a gentle image of yourself or write a poem about kindness.
4. **Journaling Improvements**
    - Keep a small diary of moments when you treated yourself with kindness. Seeing these examples in writing can prove you are capable of being supportive to yourself, no matter how you felt in the past.

Chapter 15: Handling Guilt

Guilt is a complex emotion that often goes hand-in-hand with sadness. You might feel guilty about things you have or have not done. You could worry that you have let other people down or that you have failed to meet certain standards. While guilt can sometimes be helpful if it encourages you to correct a real mistake, it can also become excessive, weighing you down and fueling sadness. In this chapter, we will discuss what guilt is, why it can grow so heavy, and ways to address it in a caring, balanced manner. We will also talk about telling the difference between useful guilt and guilt that is unfair to yourself.

Understanding Guilt

1. **Definition of Guilt**
   Guilt is the uneasy or heavy feeling that arises when you think you have done something wrong or failed to meet a responsibility. It can appear after a real mistake or even when you only *believe* you did something wrong. For instance, you might feel guilt for not being able to help a friend, or for declining an invitation because you felt too low.
2. **Why It Appears**
   - **Personal Values**: You might have internal rules or values about what is right or wrong. If you think you violated these rules, guilt can show up.
   - **Social Pressure**: Sometimes, friends, family, or society place expectations on you. If you do not meet those, you might feel guilty, even if it is not fully your fault.
   - **Depression's Influence**: Deep sadness can twist events to make you feel more responsible than you truly are. You may blame yourself for outcomes you could not control.

3. **When Guilt Is Helpful**
   Guilt can encourage you to take action. If you hurt someone's feelings by accident, guilt might remind you to apologize or try to make things right. In this sense, it can guide moral or empathic behavior.
4. **When Guilt Becomes Harmful**
   If guilt lingers for a long time or relates to things you could not have changed, it can deepen sadness. Excessive guilt can stop you from enjoying anything or seeing your self-worth clearly. You might become stuck in constant self-blame.

Why Guilt Can Become Overwhelming

1. **Assuming Full Responsibility**
   Sometimes, you blame yourself for problems that involve many factors. For example, if a group project fails, you might feel you are entirely at fault, even though other members also had roles. Depression can magnify this tendency.
2. **Overgeneralizing**
   You might take one mistake and label yourself as generally bad or irresponsible. For instance, you forget to call a friend on their birthday and then think, "I'm the worst friend ever," which goes beyond the actual slip.
3. **Past Mistakes You Cannot Undo**
   If something happened a long time ago, you may still carry guilt, replaying the event in your mind. You might wish you had acted differently or said something else. This can block you from moving forward, especially if you do not take steps to come to terms with it.
4. **External Criticism**
   If people around you blame or shame you, you can internalize those messages. This can lead you to feel guilty about things that are not truly your fault or not fully under your control.

5. **Fear of Repeating Errors**
   You may fear doing the same wrong thing again. This fear can turn into guilt even when you have not repeated the mistake, leaving you tense and worried about the future.

Identifying Real vs. Unreal Guilt

1. **Check the Facts**
   Ask yourself what actually happened. Did you truly cause the problem? Were there other elements at play? Sometimes, listing the facts on paper can clarify your part in a situation.
2. **Assess Control**
   Think about how much control you realistically had. Could you have prevented the event, or were you a small piece in a much bigger puzzle? Understanding the limits of your control can lighten unjust guilt.
3. **Distinguish Regret from Guilt**
   - **Regret**: Feeling sad something happened or wishing it were different.
   - **Guilt**: Feeling personally responsible and blaming yourself.
     Sometimes, you might feel regret without actually bearing blame.
4. **Consider Intent**
   Did you intentionally do something unkind, or were you trying your best at the time? If your intentions were not harmful, it might be a signal you are judging yourself too harshly.

Steps to Ease Guilt

1. **Apologize or Make Amends If Needed**
   If you genuinely harmed someone, consider offering a sincere

apology. Ask if there is something you can do to make up for it, within reason. This can ease the guilt by taking direct action.

2. **Learn and Grow**

   Even if you cannot change the past, you can reflect on what went wrong and see how to do better in the future. Focusing on personal growth can shift guilt into a constructive guide rather than a burden.

3. **Self-Forgiveness**

   As discussed in previous chapters, forgive yourself by recognizing that everyone makes mistakes. You can still be a good person who did something imperfect. Holding onto endless guilt blocks you from healthier emotions.

4. **Talk About It**

   Sharing guilty feelings with a trusted friend, family member, or counselor can provide a fresh viewpoint. Sometimes, hearing someone else say, "You're not fully at fault" or "You did your best" helps you let go of guilt.

Handling Guilt Tied to Depression

1. **Recognize Depression's Voice**

   Depression can convince you that everything wrong is your fault. Question these thoughts by asking if they match reality. Remind yourself that depression often paints a darker picture than the facts justify.

2. **Separate Feelings from Facts**

   You might *feel* 100% guilty, but that feeling alone does not prove you are. Distinguish emotional intensity from the actual situation. Use a journal or conversation with a friend to see if your guilt aligns with the facts.

3. **Practice Compassionate Thoughts**

   If you catch yourself saying, "It's all my fault," try shifting to, "I

feel responsible, but let me see what part I truly played."
Gentle language can reduce the grip of guilt on your mind.
4. **Seek Professional Help When Overwhelming**
If guilt is severe, causing you to withdraw from life or harming your mental health, a therapist or counselor can help. They have strategies to address negative thinking patterns that fuel unnecessary guilt.

Guilt Over Personal Feelings

1. **Feeling Bad for Being Sad**
Sometimes, you might even feel guilty about being depressed, as if you are letting others down. This is unfair guilt because you did not choose to feel low. Instead, you are managing a condition that is already challenging.
2. **Guilt for Needing Help**
Asking for support can spark guilt if you worry about burdening others. Remember, people often want to help. Accepting help does not make you weak or selfish. It simply means you recognize when you cannot handle everything alone.
3. **Worrying About Letting People Down**
You might believe that others expect you to be cheerful or productive all the time. In truth, real friends or caring family understand that everyone struggles sometimes. Feeling guilty for not always being "okay" is harsh on yourself.
4. **Saying "No" or Setting Limits**
Turning down an invitation or a request can lead to guilt if you think you should always be available. But respecting your own limits is vital (we will talk more about this in Chapter 16). Guilt for safeguarding your well-being is misplaced.

Techniques to Work Through Guilt

1. **Write a Letter to Yourself**
   - **Content**: Describe what you feel guilty about, then write a response as if you are a kind friend looking at the situation.
   - **Benefit**: This helps you see both the emotion and a gentler viewpoint. You could also safely "release" the letter by storing it away or tearing it up if you no longer need it.
2. **Role-Playing a Conversation**
   - **Method**: If you feel guilty about something you did to a person, imagine talking to them calmly. Explain your feelings and your regrets. Then imagine how a caring or fair person might respond.
   - **Reason**: This can lessen guilt by letting you mentally practice discussing the issue or find closure if it is too late to talk in real life.
3. **Check the "Guilt Scale"**
   - **Process**: Give your guilt a rating from 1 (mild) to 10 (overwhelming). Then list reasons for that rating. Next, question if that rating is fair, or if it should be higher or lower based on facts.
   - **Goal**: This stops you from automatically accepting the highest level of guilt. It encourages rational thinking.
4. **Mindful Reflection**
   - **Practice**: Sit quietly, take deep breaths, and focus on the present moment. Gently acknowledge the guilt but do not let it dominate your entire attention.
   - **Why**: Mindfulness can help you see guilt as a feeling passing through rather than something that defines who you are.

Seeking Closure for Old Guilt

1. **Consider an Apology (If Safe and Appropriate)**
   - If the person you hurt is still in your life and it is safe to contact them, you might offer a short apology. State what you are sorry for and avoid excuses. Be sincere but not self-punishing.
2. **Rituals of Release**
   - If direct contact is not possible or helpful, you can create a small personal ritual: write down the event, reflect on what you learned, then burn or tear up the paper. Symbolically letting it go can bring an emotional release.
3. **Talk with a Professional**
   - Deep, long-standing guilt—especially related to past traumas—can be tricky to solve alone. A mental health professional can guide you through safe ways to process those old events and move forward.
4. **Accepting Incomplete Resolution**
   - Sometimes you cannot fix a past mistake fully, especially if another person is no longer around or if it is too risky to contact them. In these cases, focusing on what you can learn and how you can live better from now on becomes key.

Balancing Self-Responsibility with Self-Kindness

1. **Own Your Part—Not the Entire Burden**
   - A balanced view means you admit your role in what went wrong but do not take on blame for things out of your hands. Depression can blur this line, so be firm about what you did and did not cause.
2. **Honor Your Values**

- If you value honesty, kindness, or responsibility, use guilt as a signpost. Let it remind you to stay true to those values, but do not let it become a weapon against yourself.
3. **Release What You Cannot Fix**
    - There is a limit to how much you can make amends or change a past error. If you have done what you can—such as apologizing or learning from it—further guilt only drags you down.
4. **Stay Aware of Your Humanity**
    - Mistakes are part of being human. Most people have at least a few regrets or moments they wish they could do over. You are not alone in messing up sometimes.

Examples of Situations and Approaches

1. **Feeling Guilty About a Broken Friendship**
    - **Scenario**: You stopped talking to a friend during a tough period. Now you feel guilty for cutting them off.
    - **Approach**: You might consider sending a simple message saying you are sorry for the silence and explaining that you were going through a hard time. If they respond, you can try to rebuild. If not, you can still learn to accept what happened and treat yourself with care.
2. **Guilt from Academic or Work Failure**
    - **Scenario**: You did poorly on a big test or a project at work. You blame yourself for not studying or preparing enough.
    - **Approach**: Apologize if you let down a team, or talk to a teacher or boss about how to improve. Find new study or work strategies. Remind yourself that one failure does not define your overall ability.
3. **Guilt Over Family Disagreements**

- **Scenario**: You argued with family members and said hurtful words. Now you regret it deeply.
- **Approach**: Offer a genuine apology, mentioning what you wish you had done differently. Then focus on building healthier communication. Understand that family tensions are often shared responsibilities, not just yours alone.

4. **Feeling Guilty About Self-Care**
   - **Scenario**: You took time off to rest due to depression, but you feel guilty that you were not "productive."
   - **Approach**: Recognize that resting is necessary when you are low. Remind yourself that self-care is part of maintaining health, and that skipping it could lead to bigger problems later.

Helping Others While Dealing with Your Own Guilt

1. **Avoid Overcompensating**
   - If you feel guilty, you might try to do too much for others. This can lead to burnout. Balance caring for people with caring for yourself.
2. **Be Honest About Your Limits**
   - If someone asks for help and you cannot provide it without harming your own well-being, gently explain that you wish you could, but you are not in a position to do so. Feeling guilty for saying "no" might surface, but setting limits can protect your mental health.
3. **Sharing What You Learned**
   - If you overcame guilt over a certain issue, you might help someone facing a similar situation by sharing insights. Just ensure you do not ignore your own healing to focus solely on others.
4. **Supportive Listening**

- Sometimes, simply being there for someone else's problems can help both of you feel less isolated. Be mindful of not taking on guilt for their struggles, though—you can listen without owning their burden.

Avoiding Guilt Spirals

1. **What Is a Guilt Spiral?**
    - A pattern where a single guilty thought leads to more and more self-blame, until you feel extremely distressed. Example: "I forgot to call my friend" becomes "I'm a terrible friend," then "I mess up everything," and so on.
2. **How to Break It**
    - **Interrupt the Thought**: Notice when you start piling on more accusations. Take a mental "time-out."
    - **Use Logic**: Ask, "Is this new self-blame truly linked to the original event, or am I just adding it?"
    - **Reach Out**: A quick call or text to someone supportive can pull you out of that spiral by getting an outside perspective.
3. **Set a Time Limit**
    - If guilt arises frequently, you could try scheduling a specific "worry or guilt" check-in time—maybe 5 minutes a day. If a guilty thought pops up outside that window, remind yourself you will address it later. This keeps it from dominating the entire day.
4. **Refocus on Action**
    - Guilt can paralyze you, but moving toward action—like a small apology or a practical fix—can shift your mindset from blame to resolution.

Growing Beyond Guilt

1. **Acceptance of Imperfection**
   - Accepting that you cannot always be in control or always be correct helps reduce guilt. You are a learning, changing individual.
2. **Improving Empathy**
   - Sometimes, feeling guilt can expand your empathy for others who make mistakes. You realize how painful it can be to blame yourself, so you become gentler toward others' errors as well.
3. **Rewriting Your Inner Story**
   - If your mind's story is "I'm always messing up," try adjusting it to something more truthful: "I have made mistakes, but I also have good qualities and have done positive things." This rebalanced viewpoint helps you see beyond guilt.
4. **Confidence and Growth**
   - Overcoming specific guilty feelings and resolving past issues can boost your self-trust. You realize that even if you slip again, you have tools to address the guilt and keep going.

Chapter 16: Speaking Up and Creating Limits

One reason sadness can worsen is feeling that your needs or boundaries are not respected. You may give more time, energy, or resources than you actually have, hoping to please others or avoid conflict. This can lead to exhaustion, resentment, or guilt. Learning to speak up about what you can handle—and what you cannot—is important for emotional health. This chapter will focus on finding ways to be assertive without being unkind, explaining why setting limits can reduce stress and guilt, and offering practical tips on communicating your needs calmly. We will also talk about how to handle pushback from people who resist your efforts to create healthier boundaries.

Why Limits Matter

1. **Protects Emotional Energy**
   You have a limited amount of mental and emotional energy. If you constantly say "yes" to extra tasks or demands, you can drain yourself, leaving little energy to care for your own well-being or manage sadness.
2. **Reduces Resentment**
   Without clear boundaries, you might feel taken advantage of. Over time, this can build anger or bitterness. Setting limits upfront helps maintain healthier, more honest relationships.
3. **Prevents Overload and Guilt**
   When you agree to everything, you risk failing to deliver on your promises, which can spark guilt or shame. By stating your boundaries clearly, you only commit to what is realistic.
4. **Enhances Self-Respect**
   Speaking your needs can be a form of self-kindness. By acknowledging your limitations, you show yourself and others that your well-being matters, too.

Understanding Different Boundaries

1. **Physical Boundaries**
   These involve personal space and physical touch. For example, deciding who can hug you or enter your room without knocking.
2. **Emotional Boundaries**
   These relate to what personal information you share and how people talk to you. For instance, you might limit how much someone can yell at you or judge your feelings.
3. **Time Boundaries**
   This is about how you allocate your hours. If you need alone time to recharge, saying "no" to certain invitations or tasks can protect that.
4. **Resource Boundaries**
   You might have to limit how much money or items you lend, or how frequently you do favors, so that you do not end up in financial or personal hardship.

Being Assertive vs. Aggressive

1. **Assertive**
   - **Definition**: Calmly stating your point of view, needs, or boundaries. Assertiveness respects both yourself and the other person.
   - **Example**: Saying, "I understand you need help, but I have a tight schedule this week. I can only help for 30 minutes on Saturday."
2. **Aggressive**
   - **Definition**: Forcing your view or needs on someone else in a hostile way. It might include shouting or belittling.
   - **Example**: Yelling, "Don't bother me! I have no time for you!" without any courtesy or explanation.

3. **Passive**
    - **Definition**: Not stating your needs at all, letting others walk over your boundaries. This often leads to built-up anger or guilt.
    - **Example**: Saying "yes" to extra work even though you are exhausted, feeling too afraid to refuse.
4. **Passive-Aggressive**
    - **Definition**: Indirectly expressing anger or frustration, often through sarcasm or sabotage, instead of direct communication.
    - **Example**: Saying "Sure, I'll help" while rolling your eyes, then doing a poor job out of resentment.

Assertiveness is a middle path: you do not attack others, and you do not ignore your own needs. You speak up respectfully and firmly.

Signs You Need Stronger Limits

1. **Constant Fatigue**
   If you are always exhausted, it may be because you rarely say "no." Your schedule might be overloaded with tasks for others, leaving little rest time.
2. **Frequent Anger or Resentment**
   If you catch yourself feeling upset with people for asking things of you, or if you dread their requests, that is a hint you are not speaking up about your limits.
3. **Difficulty Focusing on Your Needs**
   When you never have time for your own self-care, hobbies, or even basic rest, it might be because you have not established clear boundaries about your time.
4. **Ongoing Guilt for Saying "No"**
   If you feel intense guilt every time you refuse a request, it might be a sign you are not comfortable protecting your own

well-being. Learning to set boundaries can help reduce that guilt over time.

Steps to Speak Up

1. **Know Your Limits First**
   - **Self-Reflection**: Ask yourself how much time, energy, or emotional bandwidth you actually have. Do you need a quiet evening every day? Do you have extra capacity to help someone for an hour but not more?
   - **Example**: If you realize you need at least an hour alone each night to wind down, that becomes a boundary to communicate.
2. **Choose the Right Moment**
   - **Tip**: Bring up your needs in a calm setting if possible. Avoid times when you or the other person is very stressed or rushed.
   - **Example**: Instead of waiting until you are already burned out, plan a short talk when both parties can listen.
3. **Use Clear, Simple Language**
   - **Tip**: State what you need without long apologies or blame. Get to the point gently.
   - **Example**: "I appreciate you thinking of me, but I need to say 'no' this time. I don't have enough energy to do this task well."
4. **Acknowledge the Other Person's View**
   - **Reason**: This shows respect and can make them feel heard. However, do not let it overshadow your own limit.
   - **Example**: "I see that this project is important to you. Right now, I can't help because I'm already at my limit."

Handling Pushback

1. **Stay Firm and Calm**
   - If someone tries to argue or pressure you, repeat your boundary. Do not feel you must explain in great detail. Sticking to a brief statement can be enough.
   - **Example**: "I'm sorry, but my schedule simply won't allow it. I won't be able to do that."
2. **Offer Alternatives If You Can**
   - Sometimes, you might suggest a smaller way to help if that feels okay. If not, it is fine to just say "no."
   - **Example**: "I can't drive you there, but I can help you find bus routes or arrange a ride-share."
3. **Accept Negative Reactions**
   - Some people do not like it when you set new boundaries, especially if they benefited from you never saying "no" before. They might be upset, but that does not mean you are wrong for protecting your limits.
   - **Example**: If they say, "You're being so mean," you can calmly respond, "I'm not trying to be unkind. I just do not have the capacity right now."
4. **Know When to Walk Away**
   - If someone becomes aggressive or insulting, you can end the conversation. You do not owe them endless debate about your personal limits.
   - **Example**: "I can see we are not reaching an agreement. Let's pause this talk for now."

Communicating with Different Groups

1. **Family**
   - **Challenge**: Family members might feel entitled to your time or resources. They might guilt-trip you for not fulfilling certain roles.

- **Approach**: Gently remind them of your needs and why you must set a boundary. Emphasize that you value the relationship but also need space or rest.
2. **Friends**
   - **Challenge**: Friends may get hurt if you decline invitations. They could worry you no longer like them.
   - **Approach**: Reassure them you appreciate the friendship. Explain that your refusal is not personal but due to your current situation (stress, low mood, busy schedule).
3. **Work or School**
   - **Challenge**: Employers or teachers might assign extra duties, or classmates might expect you to carry group projects.
   - **Approach**: Clarify what you can do realistically, and what is beyond your capacity. Suggest alternatives or ask about workload adjustments if needed.
4. **Romantic Partners**
   - **Challenge**: Partners might expect you to be available for emotional support at all times. If you do not express your own limit, you could become emotionally drained.
   - **Approach**: Use honest, calm communication about how much support you can offer. If you need alone time, say so kindly but firmly.

Overcoming Common Fears

1. **Fear of Rejection**
   - You might worry that if you say "no," the other person will stop liking or respecting you. In healthy relationships, people accept each other's boundaries. If they do not, that relationship may be imbalanced.
2. **Fear of Guilt**

- If you are used to pleasing everyone, refusing can trigger guilt. Remind yourself that your well-being matters. You cannot give what you do not have.
3. **Fear of Conflict**
   - Conflict can be uncomfortable. However, setting boundaries calmly is not about creating a fight—it is about preventing future misunderstandings or resentments.
4. **Fear of Appearing "Selfish"**
   - Caring for yourself is not the same as being selfish. Selfishness means ignoring others' needs entirely. Setting a fair limit means you respect your needs while still valuing the relationship.

Practical Ways to Say "No"

1. **Direct "No"**
   - **Example**: "No, I'm sorry, but I'm not available to do that."
   - **Reason**: Simple and firm. You do not need to provide a lengthy excuse if you do not want to.
2. **Softening with Appreciation**
   - **Example**: "Thank you for asking, but I have to say no this time."
   - **Reason**: Shows you value their invitation or request, yet you still maintain your boundary.
3. **Offer a Different Option**
   - **Example**: "I can't do X, but I could do Y if that helps."
   - **Reason**: Good when you still want to assist in a smaller way without overcommitting.
4. **Delay**
   - **Example**: "Let me check my schedule and get back to you."

- **Reason**: Buys you time to think before automatically agreeing. Just be sure to actually get back to them.

Building Confidence in Speaking Up

1. **Start Small**
    - If being direct is scary, practice with minor things: decline a small favor or request first. Over time, you gain courage for bigger boundaries.
2. **Role-Play**
    - Talk with a friend or write down what you plan to say. Practicing phrases in your head or out loud can reduce nerves when the real situation comes.
3. **Reward Yourself Internally**
    - When you successfully set a limit, note how it felt afterward. You might feel relief or pride for asserting yourself. Recognizing that feeling can motivate you to keep using your voice.
4. **Seek Support**
    - If you struggle, talk to someone you trust—a counselor, a friend, or a family member—about the difficulty. They can offer tips or encouragement.

Respecting Others' Boundaries

1. **Two-Way Street**
    - Expect that if you set boundaries, others might do the same. Try to respect their "no" when they cannot meet your request. This mutual respect strengthens healthy connections.
2. **Avoid Double Standards**

- If you ask people to honor your limits, do not push them beyond theirs. Consistency builds trust and mutual care.
3. **Communicate When Boundaries Clash**
    - Sometimes, your needs and someone else's needs conflict. Calmly discuss how to compromise or find a middle ground.
4. **Honor Privacy**
    - If a friend does not want to share personal details, accept it. Just as you have the right to keep some things private, so do they.

Handling Emotional Reactions

1. **Sadness or Guilt After Saying "No"**
    - It is normal to feel a pang of sadness or guilt if you are not used to declining. Remind yourself why you had to set this boundary. Realize that feelings pass, and you are protecting your well-being.
2. **Anger from Others**
    - Someone might accuse you of being cold or rude. Keep your tone calm, restate your boundary, and avoid turning it into a shouting match. You can acknowledge their feelings but stay firm on your limit.
3. **Disappointment**
    - Even if the request was harmless, you might see disappointment in the other person's face when you say "no." Remember, it is not your job to make everyone happy at the expense of your mental health.
4. **Worry About Losing Relationships**
    - If setting healthy boundaries leads someone to end the relationship, that might indicate the relationship was conditional on you always saying "yes." While it is

painful, it can be healthier in the long run to have ties that respect your well-being.

Time Management and Scheduling Boundaries

1. **Use a Planner or Calendar**
    - Track your events, tasks, and free time. When someone asks you for a favor, look at your schedule. If it is already full, you have concrete evidence to refuse politely.
2. **Limit "Overbooking"**
    - Do not fill every single hour with tasks or social events. Keep some empty blocks for rest or last-minute needs. This buffer helps you avoid sudden overload.
3. **Have a Cutoff Time**
    - Decide on a time of day after which you will not take new requests or handle tasks. For example, after 8 p.m., you might focus on winding down, so you refuse any late-night obligations.
4. **Batch Similar Tasks**
    - Group errands or chores together so you do not have scattered tasks throughout the day. This can reduce stress and create a natural boundary around your work time versus personal time.

Special Situations

1. **Helping Loved Ones with Big Needs**
    - Sometimes, a family member or close friend truly needs substantial help (e.g., due to illness). You might choose to give more time than usual. But still keep

watch on your own limits, seeking help from other resources if needed.

2. **Living with Someone Who Pushes Boundaries**
   - If you share a home with someone who rarely respects your privacy or downtime, you may need repeated conversations or outside mediation. In serious cases, you might consider changing your living situation for your own peace.
3. **Workplace Pressure**
   - Bosses or coworkers might expect you to go beyond standard duties. If it becomes exploitative or too stressful, consider talking to a supervisor or HR about workload. If that fails, looking for a more balanced job might be an option.
4. **Cultural or Social Norms**
   - In some cultures, saying "no" can be frowned upon. Try to find polite, culturally acceptable ways to show you cannot take on certain things. This might require gentle language or seeking an intermediary to help communicate your boundary.

Signs You Are Successfully Creating Limits

1. **Less Overwhelm**
   - You notice you feel less rushed or frantic. You have more pockets of time to breathe or focus on self-care.
2. **Clearer Communication**
   - People around you start understanding what to expect from you. There is less confusion or last-minute demands.
3. **Reduced Resentment**
   - You feel less anger toward others for "invading" your time, because you now speak up before it gets too far.
4. **More Energy for Positive Things**

- By preserving your resources, you can invest in activities that brighten your mood—like creative expression, exercising, or resting peacefully.

Combining Boundaries with Other Depression-Management Tools

1. **Healthy Routines**
   - When you have a set time for work, relaxation, and sleep (as discussed in earlier chapters), it becomes easier to define your availability. You can say, "I do not schedule calls after 9 p.m. because that is my wind-down time."
2. **Self-Kindness**
   - Remind yourself that your boundaries are a reflection of caring for your mind and body, not an act of neglecting others. This stance reduces guilt and supports the kinder view of self.
3. **Supportive Relationships**
   - If you have friends or family who respect your boundaries, lean on them for encouragement. It can strengthen your resolve when dealing with less understanding people.
4. **Professional Guidance**
   - If certain relationships or tasks repeatedly override your boundaries, consider talking to a counselor. They can help you practice assertive communication or plan strategies to handle complex situations.

Chapter 17: Professional Support

When sadness or hopelessness feels heavy day after day, it can be hard to find your way alone. Friends and family may offer sympathy, but sometimes you need someone with specialized training to guide you to practical tools and deeper understanding. This is where professional support can play a key part. Many professionals are trained to help people with depression, including counselors, psychologists, psychiatrists, and social workers. Each can bring different skills and methods. In this chapter, we will look at the range of professional support options, what to expect from them, how to choose the right fit for your situation, and why it is not a sign of weakness to ask for extra help. We will also discuss how to prepare for visits, handle worries about cost, and make the most of these resources.

Understanding Different Types of Professionals

1. **Counselors or Therapists**
     - **Who They Are**: Often have a master's degree or similar training in mental health counseling, marriage and family therapy, or a related field.
     - **What They Do**: They talk with you about your feelings and problems, help you learn coping skills, and encourage personal growth. They may use specific methods like cognitive behavioral therapy (CBT) or interpersonal therapy.
     - **Why They Help**: They provide a safe, non-judgmental space for you to express yourself. They can guide you to see patterns in your thoughts or actions and suggest ways to handle stress or sadness.
2. **Psychologists**

- **Who They Are**: Specialists with a doctoral degree (Ph.D. or Psy.D.) in psychology.
- **What They Do**: They study how people think, feel, and behave. Some focus on research, while many practice psychotherapy (talk therapy). They are trained to diagnose mental health concerns using interviews, tests, and tools.
- **Why They Help**: Psychologists can use evidence-based therapies for depression, anxiety, or other struggles. They might also conduct assessments if needed for learning or mental health issues.

3. **Psychiatrists**
   - **Who They Are**: Medical doctors (M.D. or D.O.) who specialize in mental health.
   - **What They Do**: They can diagnose, treat, and prescribe medication for conditions like depression. Some also provide therapy, though many focus on managing medication while referring you to a counselor for regular talk sessions.
   - **Why They Help**: Because they have a medical background, psychiatrists can consider physical factors that might affect your mood. They can adjust or change medications if needed and keep track of side effects.

4. **Social Workers**
   - **Who They Are**: Often have a master's degree in social work (MSW) and may be licensed as clinical social workers (LCSW).
   - **What They Do**: Provide therapy, help you find resources in the community, and support you in dealing with challenges like housing or insurance. Some social workers specialize in mental health counseling.
   - **Why They Help**: They can offer emotional support and also guide you to practical services. Their approach

often looks at your environment—family, community, work—to find real-world solutions and emotional care.
5. **Other Support Roles**
    - **Nurses, Care Coordinators, Peer Specialists**: Some clinics have teams of mental health workers who handle different parts of your care. Peer specialists may have personal experience with depression and offer understanding and tips from their own path to feeling better.

When to Seek Professional Support

1. **Prolonged Sadness**
    - If you have felt down for more than a couple of weeks and it does not seem to ease, it is a good idea to talk to a professional. They can assess whether it is depression and offer early support.
2. **Difficulty Handling Daily Tasks**
    - If showering, eating, or going to school or work feel overwhelming, professional help can break that cycle. They can suggest step-by-step methods or therapies to build your strength.
3. **Thoughts of Harm**
    - Any thoughts of wanting to harm yourself or feeling life is not worth living are serious warning signs. Seeking immediate professional help is vital. Hotlines, hospital emergency departments, or crisis centers can provide urgent care.
4. **Reduced Interest in Activities**
    - Losing pleasure in all or most activities can be a sign of deeper sadness. A counselor or psychologist can help you explore why this is happening and find ways to re-engage.
5. **Advice from Loved Ones**

- Sometimes, friends or family may notice changes in your mood or behavior before you do. If they express worry and suggest you speak to a professional, consider taking their advice.

What to Expect in a First Appointment

1. **Warm Introduction**
   - Many therapists or counselors start by explaining confidentiality: what you share is private (except in special cases like risk of serious harm). They will likely ask about your main concerns.
2. **Sharing Your Story**
   - You might talk about how you have been feeling, changes in your life, how long the sadness has lasted, and what triggers it. The professional may ask questions about your health, family, or daily routines.
3. **Goal Setting**
   - A good therapist often asks what you hope to achieve. Maybe you want to sleep better, feel less hopeless, or learn to manage stress more effectively. Goals can be big or small, giving direction to the sessions.
4. **Treatment Options**
   - The professional might discuss possible therapies or approaches. For instance, cognitive behavioral therapy aims to shift negative thoughts, while interpersonal therapy focuses on improving relationship skills.
5. **Duration of Therapy**
   - Some sessions can be short-term, maybe 6 to 12 sessions, if your depression is mild. Others might go on longer if your sadness is more severe or if you want continued support over time.

Methods Professionals Might Use

1. **Cognitive Behavioral Therapy (CBT)**
   - **Focus**: Identifying and changing negative thought patterns. You learn to spot automatic, harmful thoughts and replace them with more balanced ones.
   - **Why It Helps**: It is evidence-based and can work relatively quickly. Many people see improvements in mood by practicing CBT exercises between sessions.
2. **Interpersonal Therapy**
   - **Focus**: Building healthier relationships and improving communication. This can address conflicts, grief, or changes in social roles that contribute to sadness.
   - **Why It Helps**: Depression can deepen when you feel isolated or have tension with loved ones. Interpersonal therapy fosters better support and understanding.
3. **Psychodynamic Therapy**
   - **Focus**: Looking into deeper patterns, often formed in early life, which may shape current feelings or actions. It tries to bring hidden conflicts or past hurts to the surface.
   - **Why It Helps**: By understanding root causes, you can change long-standing emotional responses and gain insight into who you are.
4. **Solution-Focused Therapy**
   - **Focus**: Finding practical, immediate steps rather than delving into deep past issues. It guides you to recognize your strengths and develop small, achievable goals.
   - **Why It Helps**: If you want quick, action-based methods, this approach can offer relief. It often builds hope by highlighting small successes.
5. **Medication Management**

- **Provided By**: Psychiatrists (or sometimes nurse practitioners) who can prescribe antidepressants or other medicines.
- **Why It Helps**: For moderate to severe depression, medication can balance brain chemistry. Many people use medication along with therapy to get the best outcome.

Handling Concerns About Medication

1. **Common Worries**
    - Some fear they will lose their personality or become dependent on medication. Others worry about side effects or the idea of needing pills to feel better.
2. **Fact-Checking**
    - Antidepressants do not make you a different person; they adjust certain brain chemicals. Side effects vary, but they can often be managed by adjusting the type or dose.
3. **Patience**
    - Medication can take a few weeks to show effects. It might also take a couple of tries to find the right medication that suits your body. Regular check-ins with the prescribing doctor help ensure safety.
4. **Combining with Therapy**
    - Medication alone sometimes eases symptoms, but therapy can provide practical coping skills. Many doctors suggest using both for a more thorough approach.
5. **You Have a Voice**
    - If you dislike how a medication feels or if side effects become bothersome, tell your psychiatrist. You can discuss switching to another type or exploring other treatments. It is a shared decision.

Cost and Accessibility

1. **Insurance Coverage**
     - If you have health insurance, check your plan for mental health benefits. Many plans must cover therapy or counseling. You might have copays or deductibles to pay out of pocket, but the insurance can cover part of the cost.
2. **Sliding Scale Fees**
     - Some therapists adjust their fees based on your income. If you cannot pay the full fee, ask if they have a sliding scale option.
3. **Community Clinics**
     - Nonprofit or government-funded clinics often offer lower-cost or free counseling. Look up local mental health centers in your area. They may have a waiting list, so it helps to contact them early.
4. **Online Therapy**
     - More professionals now provide virtual sessions by video or phone. This can save travel time and sometimes cost, though coverage varies. Check if you feel comfortable with online sessions.
5. **University Clinics**
     - If you are a student, see if your school offers free or low-cost counseling. Some universities also run training clinics where students in advanced programs provide therapy under supervision at reduced prices.

How to Find the Right Professional

1. **Ask for Recommendations**
     - Friends, family, or doctors might suggest someone they trust. If you feel safe asking, see if they know a

good counselor. Word of mouth can help find a comfortable match.
2. **Use Online Directories**
    - Websites like the Psychology Today directory (in some regions) let you filter therapists by specialty, location, insurance accepted, and more. Look for those who list depression as an area they commonly treat.
3. **Check Credentials**
    - A licensed mental health professional has met certain educational and ethical standards. You can look for letters like LPC, LCSW, LMFT, Psy.D., or M.D. (psychiatrist).
4. **Initial Phone Call or Email**
    - Many therapists are open to a brief chat or email exchange to discuss your concerns, their methods, and their fee. This can help you sense if you might click with them.
5. **Personal Fit Matters**
    - Feeling safe and understood by your therapist is important. If after a few sessions you do not feel you can open up or trust them, it is okay to seek someone else. Therapists understand that not every match is perfect.

Making the Most of Therapy

1. **Show Up Regularly**
    - Consistency helps therapy gain momentum. Skipping many sessions can slow progress. Even if you feel low or unmotivated, try to attend. That session might be the one that makes a difference.
2. **Be Open and Honest**
    - Talking about personal feelings can be uncomfortable at first. But the more honest you are, the better your

counselor can help. Share difficult thoughts, even if they seem dark or strange.
3. **Do Homework or Practice Skills**
    - Therapists might suggest writing in a journal, trying relaxation exercises, or noting your moods. Doing these tasks between sessions helps you apply new insights to real life.
4. **Speak Up About Goals**
    - If there is something specific you want to work on, let your therapist know. Maybe you want to handle guilt better, communicate more clearly with family, or manage anxious thoughts. Clear goals shape the direction of therapy.
5. **Review Progress Periodically**
    - Every so often, ask yourself and your therapist how things are going. Are you seeing some relief from sadness? Do you have new coping methods? If you feel stuck, talk about adjusting the approach.

Handling Stigma or Fear of Judgement

1. **Recognize Unfair Labels**
    - Some people still hold old-fashioned ideas about therapy, thinking it is only for very severe cases or that it means you are "weak." In reality, many individuals from all walks of life benefit from counseling.
2. **Your Health Is Private**
    - You do not have to share that you are seeing a therapist with everyone. It is your personal choice whom to tell. A mental health appointment is as valid as going to a dentist for a toothache.
3. **Look for Positive Voices**

       - More people are speaking openly about mental health care. You can find supportive online groups or public figures who talk about using therapy. This can reduce any sense of isolation or shame.
4. **Use Your Own Words**
     - If you do talk about therapy, focus on how it is helping you manage stress, learn new skills, or ease your sadness. Emphasize that it is a normal part of taking care of yourself.

Crisis Support and Hotlines

1. **Emergency Lines**
     - If you ever feel unsafe or are close to harming yourself, call emergency services (like 911 in some countries) or go to the nearest hospital. Safety must come first.
2. **Hotlines**
     - Many places have 24/7 phone lines staffed by trained volunteers or mental health workers. For instance, in the U.S., dialing or texting 988 connects you to a mental health crisis line. Other countries have similar services. These lines can offer immediate help or guide you to local resources.
3. **Text or Chat Services**
     - Some crisis services let you text or chat online if phone calls feel too hard. This can be especially helpful for younger people or those uncomfortable with speaking aloud about their feelings.
4. **You Are Not Alone**
     - Remember that calling a hotline is not an overreaction. People working there exist specifically to support callers in distress. They want to listen and help you find calm or next steps.

Cultural or Language Considerations

1. **Finding Culturally Aware Therapists**
   - If you prefer someone who understands your cultural background or speaks your native language, look for therapists who list cultural competence or multilingual skills.
   - This can help you feel more understood regarding family expectations or cultural beliefs that might affect how you experience sadness.
2. **Addressing Traditions**
   - In some cultures, mental health issues are rarely discussed openly. You might fear how your community will react if they learn you are seeking therapy. A culturally sensitive professional can help you handle this aspect while still receiving care.
3. **Interpreters**
   - If you speak a different language, ask if the clinic provides interpreters or if your insurance covers that. Some agencies have phone interpretation options for therapy sessions.
4. **Respect for Beliefs**
   - A good counselor respects your spiritual or religious beliefs. If you find that a therapist dismisses these or tries to change them, you might search for someone who aligns better with your worldview.

Online and Telehealth Options

1. **Flexibility**
   - Online therapy can remove barriers such as travel distance or scheduling difficulties. It might fit better into your routine, especially if you have limited transportation or physical challenges.

2. **Platforms**
   - Various websites or apps connect you with licensed counselors who offer video, phone, or messaging sessions. Be sure to check that the platform is secure and the therapists are properly licensed.
3. **Potential Downsides**
   - Online therapy might lack the in-person sense of connection. Also, insurance coverage for online sessions may vary. Technical issues or lack of privacy at home can sometimes be hurdles.
4. **Legitimacy**
   - Confirm the platform's reputation and read reviews if possible. Choose services that confirm their providers' credentials and follow confidentiality rules.

Knowing When It's Time for a New Approach

1. **Feeling Stuck**
   - If you have given a particular therapist or method a fair try (usually several sessions), but you see no progress or feel more uneasy, you might consider trying someone else or a different style of therapy.
2. **Worsening Symptoms**
   - In some cases, you might realize you need medication alongside therapy or more frequent sessions to stabilize severe sadness or anxiety. Discuss your options with a doctor or psychiatrist.
3. **Changes in Life Circumstances**
   - If you move, change jobs, or shift your schedule, you could look for a therapist closer to your new location or with different availability. You can transfer your records, or the old provider may refer you to a new one.
4. **Desire for Specific Techniques**

- Suppose you want to explore a new therapy method (like EMDR for trauma, or a group therapy approach). Feel free to search for a provider who specializes in that area.

Combining Professional Help with Other Strategies

1. **Lifestyle Adjustments**
   - A therapist might remind you to keep a regular sleep schedule, eat balanced meals, and add gentle exercise (as covered in earlier chapters). These daily habits work hand-in-hand with therapy.
2. **Supportive Relationships**
   - You can share, when comfortable, some therapy insights with trusted friends or family. That way, they can understand how to better support you outside sessions.
3. **Creative Expression**
   - Professionals might encourage you to journal, draw, or make music. This aligns with methods we discussed in the chapter on arts and expression. It can help process emotions between therapy visits.
4. **Focus on Progress**
   - Over time, with professional help, you might notice changes: less hopelessness, better focus, improved ability to cope with daily stress. Reflect on these steps regularly as motivation to continue.

Acknowledging Your Courage

Reaching out for professional support is not easy. It can feel scary to open up to a stranger or to consider medication. Yet, choosing to seek help shows strength and a willingness to care for yourself. Therapists are trained to guide you at a pace that feels manageable. They do not expect you to have everything figured out. You do not have to know the "right words" to say—just be honest about your challenges and what you want to change.

Also, remember it is normal to try a few different professionals before finding someone you feel comfortable with. This does not mean you failed; it just means you are looking for a good match. Depression can cloud your view of hope, but with consistent support, many people do find relief and reach a steadier emotional ground.

Professional support is one part of a larger picture in managing depression. It often works best when combined with healthy routines, good sleep, social connections, and other techniques you have learned in earlier chapters. As you continue reading, keep in mind that you do not have to do all these things alone. A qualified counselor, psychologist, or psychiatrist can walk beside you, offering knowledge and skills tailored to your situation.

Chapter 18: Checking Progress

When you face long-term sadness, it can be hard to notice changes that occur slowly over time. You might think you are still stuck in the same unhappy place, even though you have made small improvements. Checking your progress helps you see how far you have come, and it also reveals what areas still need extra attention. This chapter covers various ways to monitor your emotional state, measure changes in mood or habits, and spot when you might need to adjust your strategies. By actively tracking your ups and downs, you gain a clearer picture of what is working and what is not. This can boost your motivation and guide you to refine your approach to managing depression.

Why Checking Progress Matters

1. **Increases Awareness**
   By paying close attention to how you feel day by day or week by week, you become more aware of improvements or warning signs. This awareness can keep you from being caught off-guard by a sudden dip or from missing small victories.
2. **Guides Adjustments**
   If you see that a certain habit (like taking a quick walk each morning) seems to improve your mood, you can keep doing it or expand on it. If another approach does not seem to help, you can replace it or change it up.
3. **Boosts Confidence**
   Tracking progress can reveal that you have made steps forward, even if you still feel low. Realizing you are not standing in the exact same place can give you hope and encourage you to keep going.

4. **Supports Communication with Professionals**
   If you are working with a counselor, psychologist, or doctor, showing them concrete notes on your mood or habits can help them tailor their advice. They see patterns more clearly and can adjust your treatment plan.

Tools for Tracking Mood and Habits

1. **Mood Diaries**
   - **How to Do It**: Set aside a few minutes each day to write down your mood (e.g., on a 1-10 scale or using words like "low," "fair," "good"). Add a quick note about any standout events or feelings.
   - **Why It Helps**: You can spot patterns like feeling worse on certain days or after certain activities. Over time, you get a broader picture of your emotional ebb and flow.
2. **Apps or Online Platforms**
   - **Examples**: Many mental health apps let you log your mood, track sleep, or even note triggers. They might provide charts showing changes over weeks or months.
   - **Benefit**: Having a visual graph can make progress or setbacks more obvious than just memory alone.
3. **Physical Health Trackers**
   - **What to Track**: Sleep hours, exercise, water intake, or even heart rate. Some people use fitness watches or phone apps.
   - **Reason**: Depression can be linked to poor sleep or low physical activity. Seeing how these factors affect your mood can highlight areas to improve.
4. **Daily Checklists**
   - **Method**: Create a simple list of tasks or self-care items (like "took a shower," "ate at least two healthy meals,"

"did a short breathing exercise"). Place a check or note next to each you complete.
- **Why**: This helps you see small successes each day. Even routine tasks can feel like big wins if you are dealing with deep sadness.

Signs of Progress

1. **Better Ability to Complete Tasks**
    - You might notice you can do chores, schoolwork, or job duties with less struggle than before. Maybe you still feel some reluctance, but not as strongly as in the past.
2. **Less Overwhelming Sadness**
    - Sadness might still be present, but it might be less intense, or last fewer hours each day. Perhaps you do not cry as often or you experience fewer negative thoughts.
3. **More Interest in Activities**
    - A key sign of improvement is regaining some spark for hobbies or social events you used to avoid. Even if the interest is mild, it can be a step up from feeling numb or disinterested in everything.
4. **Fewer Moments of Hopelessness**
    - You may still have low periods, but you might catch yourself thinking, "Maybe things can get better," or "I can handle this." That sense of possibility can be a big shift.
5. **Greater Social Connection**
    - You might find it easier to text a friend, have a short conversation, or join a small outing. This growth in social willingness often indicates reduced isolation, which ties to better emotional balance.

Recognizing Setbacks

1. **What They Are**
   - Setbacks are times when your mood or functioning dips again after some improvement. It is not unusual in managing depression to have ups and downs. A setback does not erase all progress.
2. **Why They Happen**
   - They can happen due to stress, changes in routine, life events, or even physical illnesses. Sometimes, no clear reason emerges. Depression can fluctuate.
3. **How to Respond**
   - Instead of seeing a setback as a total loss, treat it as a signal. Ask: "Did something trigger this?" or "Do I need extra rest, therapy sessions, or support right now?"
4. **Avoid Despair**
   - It is easy to feel like giving up if you slip back into sadness. But setbacks can be part of the longer process of feeling better. Use them to learn more about what you need to adjust, and reach out for help if needed.

Methods for Self-Reflection

1. **Weekly Review**
   - **How**: Pick a day of the week to look back on the previous days. Ask yourself what went well, what felt hard, and how you handled stress.
   - **Benefit**: Doing this weekly prevents your experiences from fading in your mind. You gain a sharper sense of which patterns are forming.
2. **Question Prompts**

- **Examples**: "What made me smile this week?" "What felt like a huge challenge?" "Which coping skills helped the most?"
- **Reason**: Structured questions guide your thinking so you do not just dwell on negative moments. They also highlight small positives.

3. **Comparing to Past Notes**
   - If you kept a journal or mood diary a few months ago, read an entry from that time. See if your worries or mood have shifted. You might realize you have made subtle yet real progress.
4. **Discussion with a Friend or Counselor**
   - Sometimes, talking openly helps you spot changes you did not see by yourself. A friend might say, "You are much more talkative now," or "You handle conflicts better than you did before."

Checking Changes in Thoughts and Beliefs

1. **Negative Self-Talk**
   - Are you still bombarded with thoughts like "I'm worthless," or have they become less frequent or less strong? Even a slight weakening of such thoughts can reflect progress.
2. **Catastrophic Thinking**
   - Do you still jump to worst-case scenarios instantly, or do you pause and think more calmly? Reducing this habit can lift overall anxiety and sadness.
3. **Self-Kindness**
   - Notice if you have started speaking more gently to yourself (as discussed in the chapter on self-kindness). If you catch self-blame and replace it with a fairer assessment, that is a key improvement.
4. **Sense of Hope**

- Check how often you catch yourself imagining a better future or feeling you can handle challenges. Even modest flickers of hope show your mind is open to the idea that things can improve.

Goal-Setting and Milestones

1. **Setting Realistic Goals**
   - Focus on short, doable steps, like "Take a short walk 3 times this week" or "Finish reading one chapter of a book." Achieving these small goals can show you that progress is possible.
2. **Recognizing Milestones**
   - A milestone could be going a full week without missing school or work, or being able to manage anxious feelings in a public situation. Mark these moments in your diary or share them with someone supportive.
3. **Avoiding Overly High Expectations**
   - If you set huge goals ("I must be fully happy by next month!"), you might feel failure if you do not reach them. Instead, aim for steady steps forward, understanding that healing often moves in small increments.
4. **Adjusting as You Grow**
   - As you get better at certain tasks or cope more easily, you can set new goals that challenge you slightly. For instance, if you are comfortable taking a 10-minute walk, aim for 15 minutes. Stretch yourself gently, not abruptly.

Involving Others in Your Progress

1. **Accountability Partners**
    - Ask a friend or family member to check in with you about certain habits. They could ask, "Did you manage to do your short relaxation exercise today?" This can keep you mindful of your plan.
2. **Sharing Logs with Counselors**
    - If you see a therapist, bring your mood diary or daily checklist to sessions. They can help interpret patterns and suggest changes in therapy or routines based on the data.
3. **Group Support**
    - Support groups (in person or online) can offer a space to discuss progress with others who understand sadness. Hearing their stories can motivate you and offer new ideas.

Dealing with Self-Doubt During Progress Checks

1. **"I'm Not Improving Fast Enough"**
    - You might feel impatient. Sadness can make you believe you should be "fixed" by now. But real changes can take weeks or months. Each small step matters.
2. **"It's Just a Fluke"**
    - When you see progress, depression might whisper that it is temporary. Remind yourself that even if a good day passes, it shows you can have better days again.
3. **"Other People Are Doing So Much Better"**
    - Comparing your timeline to someone else's can lead to discouragement. Everyone's path differs. Focus on your specific steps rather than measuring yourself against others.

4. **"I Shouldn't Have Setbacks"**
    - If you do slip back, you might blame yourself for not being strong enough. Realize setbacks happen to nearly everyone dealing with depression. They do not erase the growth you have made.

Signs You Might Need More Support

1. **Persistent Low Score**
    - If you are recording mood scores and they remain very low (like 2 or 3 out of 10) for multiple weeks despite trying your coping tools, it might be time to talk to a professional or revisit your treatment approach.
2. **New or Worsening Thoughts of Harm**
    - If you notice your negative thoughts become more frequent or severe, reach out immediately to a mental health professional or hotline.
3. **Physical Health Declines**
    - If changes in sleep, appetite, or general health keep getting worse, that may signal your current strategies are not enough on their own.
4. **Inability to Function**
    - Missing many days of school or work, struggling with basic tasks, or feeling too paralyzed to try coping tools are clear indicators you may need more intense help, such as a higher level of therapy, medication, or a support group.

Balancing Structured Tracking with Flexibility

1. **Avoid Over-Tracking**
    - Writing too many details every day can become stressful. If it starts to feel like a burden, consider a

simpler system. The goal is to help you notice patterns, not to overwhelm you with data entry.
2. **Stay Flexible**
    - If a certain method (like a phone app) becomes tedious, switch to a handwritten diary or vice versa. The best tool is the one you will actually use consistently.
3. **Celebrate or Mark Changes in a Gentle Way**
    - Notice progress with a sense of calm positivity. You might treat yourself to a restful break or share a smile with a friend. Keep it simple and personal.
4. **Use Tracking As a Compass**
    - If a day's mood rating is low, see it as a guide that you might need self-care or to reach out to someone. If it is high, note what helped. This turns your records into a practical tool for daily decisions.

Mindful Observation in Real Time

1. **Body Scan**
    - A few times a day, close your eyes and scan from your head to your toes. Note any tension or pain. This can help you realize if stress is building, so you can do a quick release technique.
2. **Breath Check**
    - Notice if you are breathing shallowly. If so, pause to take a few gentle deep breaths. This small action can steady your mind and also give a clue about your emotional state at that moment.
3. **Emotion Labeling**
    - When a strong feeling arises, name it: "I feel annoyed," "I feel lonely," or "I feel a small sense of happiness." Labeling can lower the intensity and help you understand your mood more precisely.

4. **Short Journaling**
   - Jot a single sentence about how you feel in the moment. If done several times a day, you gather multiple mood snapshots. This can be more detailed than a single daily summary.

Planning Changes After a Progress Check

1. **Identify One Area to Improve**
   - If your records show you skip breakfast often and it leads to low energy, for example, decide to work on that first. Setting one clear focus keeps you from feeling overwhelmed.
2. **Brainstorm Solutions**
   - Think of small ways to address the issue. Maybe plan quick meals, ask someone to remind you to eat, or place a note on the fridge. Turn your logs into actionable ideas.
3. **Try a New Strategy**
   - If you have been using the same relaxation exercise for months and see no real impact, try a different one. Or if you have not tried journaling, give it a go.
4. **Involve Allies**
   - Let a friend or counselor know what you discovered in your progress check. They can offer tips or help you refine your plan. Having a teammate in this process can keep you motivated.

Seeing Progress as an Ongoing Process

1. **No Deadline for Feeling Better**
   - Depression recovery rarely follows a neat timeline. Some people see changes in weeks, others in months

or longer. Keep the perspective that each day's step is part of a continuing path toward steadier mood.
   2. **Adapting to Life's Changes**
      - Even if you see big improvements, future stressors or events might temporarily push you back. That is normal. Having a habit of tracking can help you spot problems early and respond before things worsen.
   3. **Letting Go of Perfection**
      - You do not need to track absolutely everything or become an expert in mental health data. A balanced approach—just enough structure to get insights—is sufficient.
   4. **Recognizing Lifelong Skills**
      - The tools you use to track your mood and handle sadness can continue to support you throughout your life. Even if depression fully lifts, you can keep using self-reflection and mindful observation to handle any future emotional dips.

When to Pause Tracking

   1. **Feeling Overly Focused on Numbers**
      - If your daily mood rating becomes an obsession, causing anxiety or negative competition with yourself, it might be healthier to step back. The aim is to help, not create stress.
   2. **You Have Achieved Stable Improvement**
      - If you find yourself in a better place consistently, you might decide to track less often—maybe weekly instead of daily. As long as you remain mindful of your mood, you do not always need detailed logs.
   3. **Therapist Suggestion**
      - Sometimes, your counselor or doctor may advise a break from formal tracking if it seems to fuel

perfectionism or if you are focusing too heavily on measuring every detail.
4. **Check-Ins Instead of Daily Tracking**
    - Instead of stopping completely, you might switch to a general monthly check. This can maintain awareness without the daily or weekly detail. Stay flexible to your comfort level.

Using Results to Encourage Next Steps

1. **Share Success Stories**
    - Even if it is just with a close friend, talk about how you felt two months ago compared to now. This reflection can reinforce that you are capable of change.
2. **Plan for Larger Goals**
    - If your baseline sadness is decreasing, you can try bigger goals, like rejoining a favorite club or class you once avoided. Keep building on the foundation you have laid.
3. **Integrate More Tools**
    - Perhaps you have only been focusing on sleep and mood tracking. Now that you see results, consider adding light exercise, new hobbies, or deeper therapy techniques. Expand your coping methods step by step.
4. **Keep Revisiting**
    - As time goes on, come back to the logs or notes from early in your process. You might be pleasantly surprised by how your perspective, daily habits, or emotional tone have shifted.

Chapter 19: Keeping Steady Gains

As you have worked through sadness, you have likely tried new methods—whether it is setting routines, talking to supportive people, or practicing calm techniques. Over time, you may notice some improvement. Your mind might feel a bit lighter, your daily tasks less of a struggle, or your negative thoughts somewhat quieter. While this is encouraging, one of the biggest hurdles is figuring out how to maintain these positive changes. It is common to make progress but then slip back into old patterns if you do not have a plan to keep moving forward.

In this chapter, we will discuss how to keep steady gains once you start feeling a little better. We will look at ways to remain consistent in your new habits, handle challenging times without losing hope, and continue growing your sense of stability. These ideas include maintaining routines, nurturing supportive bonds, refining coping tools, and preparing for times when sadness creeps up again. The goal is to help you remain on a firm path instead of feeling that each improvement is temporary. By learning to hold onto your progress, you add another strong piece to your overall approach in managing depression.

Why Gains Can Slip Away

1. **Easing Off the Tools**
    - One reason progress can fade is that people drop the routines and habits they formed once they start feeling better. They might stop doing breathing exercises, journaling, or meeting with a counselor. The mind can slide back into old ruts when these supportive actions end.
2. **Unexpected Stress**

- Life does not pause just because you are healing. Problems at work, arguments with family, or sudden disappointments can arise. If you are not prepared, these stresses can overwhelm you, making it hard to maintain the progress you have made.
3. **Physical or Environmental Changes**
    - A new job, moving homes, or changes in sleeping arrangements can disrupt the stability you built. When the environment shifts, it might be challenging to keep your daily habits going.
4. **Believing You Are "Done"**
    - It is natural to want to believe that once sadness lifts a little, you will never feel that heaviness again. However, depression can be long-term and might return if you stop paying attention to your mental well-being.
5. **Self-Doubt**
    - You might worry your improvements are not real or that you do not deserve them. This doubt can chip away at your confidence. If you start thinking your good days are just accidents, it is easy to lose the willingness to keep up healthy actions.

Building Routines That Last

1. **Identify Your Core Supportive Habits**
    - Look at everything you tried—journaling, short walks, morning stretches, bedtime routines. Which ones made the biggest difference? Which felt most natural to keep doing? Focus on these first.
2. **Keep It Realistic**
    - Overly complicated routines can collapse under busy schedules or low energy days. Maybe you have a 30-minute plan that is too tough to follow each day.

Consider a lighter version—like a 10-minute walk or a 5-minute breathing pause—that you can realistically maintain.
3. **Set Daily and Weekly Checkpoints**
    - Having a simple daily checklist (such as "took vitamins," "spent 10 minutes reading something calming," "talked to a friend or relative") can keep you accountable. A weekly review—maybe on Sunday—lets you see how consistent you have been.
4. **Adjust as Needed**
    - Life changes, and your routine may have to shift with it. If your new job starts early, maybe you move your quiet reading time to lunchtime instead of the morning. The key is to adapt rather than abandon the routine.
5. **Stack Habits Together**
    - If you already have a habit—like brushing your teeth every morning—tie a new habit to it, such as doing 2 minutes of slow breathing afterward. This makes the new behavior easier to remember.

Strengthening Supportive Bonds

1. **Stay Connected to Helpful People**
    - When you are feeling a bit better, it might be tempting to isolate again, thinking you should handle everything alone now. But maintaining your gains often means continuing to have supportive friends or groups who understand. Keep in touch by sending short messages, making quick calls, or planning low-pressure meetups.
2. **Consider Group Activities or Classes**
    - If you have found partial relief from sadness, participating in a friendly group—like a gentle sports club, a book discussion group, or an art class—can

keep you socially engaged. Such activities remind you that you are part of a community and can prevent loneliness.

3. **Update People on Your Progress**
    - Let your close friends or family know when something is working for you. For instance, if writing in a journal at night helps you rest, share this insight so they can cheer you on and respect your routine.
4. **Encourage Accountability Buddies**
    - You and a friend could check in on each other's well-being. It can be as simple as a weekly text asking, "How are things going with your mood or daily routines?" This small gesture keeps you mindful that someone cares.
5. **Seek Further Guidance if Needed**
    - If you have been seeing a counselor less frequently because you felt improvement, consider scheduling a maintenance session once a month or once every two months. This gives you a space to discuss any bumps in the road before they grow.

Refining Your Coping Tools

1. **Assess What Works Best**
    - You may have tried many techniques to fight sadness: breathing exercises, replacing negative thoughts, going on short walks. Use your tracking (as discussed in Chapter 18) to see which methods gave you the most relief or stability.
2. **Go Deeper into Successful Methods**
    - If negative thinking shifts best with a certain approach (like thought-challenging or journaling), devote time to mastering that technique even more. Perhaps you can read a book or talk to a counselor about advanced ways to apply it.

3. **Combine Tools for Better Effect**
    - Sometimes, layering coping methods can strengthen your defenses against sadness. For instance, if going to bed early helps your mood, you could also add a short relaxation routine before sleep. The two actions together might give you steadier results.
4. **Keep a Backup List for Tough Days**
    - Have a written (or digital) list of quick coping actions you can use when you notice your mood dropping: a 5-minute grounding exercise, a favorite calming song, a brief walk outside, or a short call with a trusted friend. Having these ideas in one place saves you from struggling to remember them under stress.
5. **Learn New Techniques Over Time**
    - Just because you have found some strategies does not mean you cannot explore others. Maybe you have yet to try mindful coloring, progressive muscle relaxation, or guided audio exercises. Add variety to your toolbox so you do not get stuck if one method feels stale.

Handling Triggers and Challenges

1. **Identify Common Triggers**
    - A trigger is something that often worsens your sadness or negative thoughts. It might be an argument, a reminder of a past event, or even seeing certain people. Knowing your triggers means you can prepare coping plans in advance.
2. **Plan in Advance**
    - If you know a holiday gathering or a particular appointment can trigger low mood, think ahead about how to handle it. Maybe you limit your time there, bring a supportive friend, or schedule a short relaxation break afterward.

3. **Check Your "Stress Bucket"**
    - You can imagine your stress as water filling a bucket. When the bucket overflows, you feel overwhelmed. Each new stressor adds water. But using coping tools or taking breaks drains some water. Keep an eye on how full your bucket feels day to day.
4. **Practice Communication Skills**
    - When arguments or misunderstandings spark sadness, you can practice calm ways to express yourself. If needed, remind yourself to take a short pause in heated moments. Calm speech can solve problems quicker and spare you from deeper frustration.
5. **Understand Setbacks Will Happen**
    - Even with strong coping, triggers may catch you off guard sometimes. Instead of feeling like you failed, see it as part of the process. Return to your supportive tools, talk to a counselor if necessary, and keep going.

Checking In with Yourself

1. **Ongoing Mood Tracking**
    - Even if you do not do it daily, a short weekly or bi-weekly log can help. You can note: "This week, my average mood was around a 6 out of 10," or "I had one really tough day on Wednesday." It keeps you aware of any patterns.
2. **Self-Reflection Questions**
    - Ask yourself: "Am I still using the methods that helped me before?" "Have I let any helpful habits slip?" "Is there any new stress I have not dealt with?" Answering these can show where you stand.
3. **Physical Check**
    - Body and mind are linked. Notice if your neck is tense or if your shoulders are always tight. Tension might

mean you are bottling up worries. If you catch these signs early, you can do a short relaxation or breathing activity.

4. **Praise Your Efforts**
   - After you complete a tough task or handle a bad day, acknowledge that you managed it. This does not mean bragging or ignoring problems. It is simply recognizing that you put in the work. This small acknowledgment can reinforce the idea that you are capable.

5. **Compare to the Past, Not Others**
   - When seeing how far you have come, look at how you felt last month or last year. Comparing yourself to other people can be discouraging because everyone's life is unique. Focus on your own improvements, whether big or small.

Staying Motivated

1. **Plan Small Rewards or Pleasantries**
   - If you manage a challenging week, treat yourself to something comforting, like a fun read or a gentle activity you enjoy. This can encourage you to stay consistent. (Remember to keep it simple and personal, so it is not about lavish events—just a small recognition.)

2. **Visual Reminders**
   - You could have a note on your wall or phone that says, "Keep going—you have made progress before." Sometimes, reading a positive phrase can refresh your mindset when you feel low.

3. **Variety in Routine**
   - Monotony can dull your sense of progress. Change small things: walk a slightly different route, try a new recipe, or rearrange a corner of your living space. Novelty can keep you engaged in daily life.

4. **Short-Term Goals**
    - Long-term aims, like "I want to be free from depression entirely," can feel distant. Setting a short-term goal (like "This month, I will practice mindful breathing 3 times a week") is more concrete. Achieving short-term goals builds a sense of ability.
5. **Reflect on Meaning**
    - Sometimes, sadness lessens when you connect with what matters to you—whether it is faith, family, creativity, or a cause you care about. Reflect on how your improved well-being helps you take part in things that give you a sense of value.

Dealing with Relapses

1. **What Is a Relapse?**
    - A relapse is when your mood significantly drops again after a period of improvement. It can happen gradually or suddenly. You might feel old negative thoughts flooding back or lose energy for tasks that were getting easier.
2. **How to Respond**
    - Remind yourself that a relapse does not undo all the growth you achieved. You still have the knowledge and tools that got you to a better place before. Return to basics: consistent sleep, gentle exercise, supportive talk, and possibly a re-check with a counselor.
3. **Early Warning Signs**
    - Notice signals that a relapse might be forming: increased irritability, wanting to isolate, skipping meals. If you see these, take action quickly. Do not wait until you are fully overwhelmed.
4. **Reach Out Sooner Than Later**
    - Sometimes, people feel shame in returning to therapy or telling friends they are struggling again. However,

seeking help early often reduces how intense the relapse becomes.
5. **Celebrate Past Successes**
    - If you overcame a bad spell before, you can do it again. Recall that you have proven your ability to feel better, even if it took time. This memory can ground you in the fact that relapse is not the end of your progress.

Reinforcing a Healthy Mindset

1. **Balanced Perspective**
    - Part of keeping your gains is seeing your sadness as one part of you, not the whole story. You might struggle with low mood, but you also have strengths, interests, and abilities. Keep reminding yourself of these truths.
2. **Realistic Optimism**
    - Overly bright views that deny any difficulty can backfire. But a realistic optimism, which says "I have challenges, but I can do small things to feel better," supports a steady emotional state.
3. **Avoiding Extremes**
    - Watch for black-and-white thinking: "Either I'm fully well or I'm a total mess." Most people fall somewhere in between. Accepting that partial improvement is still improvement helps you hold onto hope.
4. **Gratitude Practices**
    - Some people find noting a few good moments each day (like a kind word from a friend, a small success at work, or a pleasant meal) can prevent them from dwelling on everything that went wrong. This does not deny problems but balances them with bits of positivity.
5. **Keep Learning**

- Staying curious about mental well-being encourages you to refine your approach. You can read articles, watch talks by mental health experts, or ask your counselor questions. The mind is complex, and there is always more to learn.

Living Beyond a Diagnosis

1. **You Are More Than "Depressed"**
   - A diagnosis like depression is just a label for a condition you face. It does not define you fully. Remember the hobbies you like, the roles you fill (friend, student, parent, partner), and the traits that make you unique.
2. **Balancing Self-Care with Daily Demands**
   - If you have gained momentum, you might feel ready to take on more tasks—like extra work or social events. Pace yourself. Overloading your schedule can risk burnout. Learn to say "no" when you must.
3. **Share Your Growth if You Want**
   - Telling your story can inspire others who are struggling. However, you do not owe anyone a detailed account unless you choose. Keep some boundaries to protect your own peace.
4. **Keep a Lifeline of Support**
   - Even if you consider yourself mostly out of deep sadness, maintaining occasional check-ins with a counselor or a supportive friend can be a safety net. If new stress arises, you already have a place to turn.
5. **Think in Terms of Ongoing Care**
   - Just as someone with a physical condition might monitor their diet or take medicine long-term, people with a history of deep sadness often continue small protective actions indefinitely. This is normal and wise.

Chapter 20: Hope for the Future

Having walked through deep sadness, tried supportive methods, built healthier routines, and learned how to hold onto any progress, you may wonder what comes next. Is it possible to find genuine hope after feeling so low for so long? Hope can be tricky when depression tries to convince you that nothing will change. Yet hope is the sense that tomorrow can be different from today—that you can still find joy or meaning even if life has been hard.

This final chapter will explore what hope can mean after dealing with depression. We will look at why hope is not simply wishful thinking but a practical stance that fuels ongoing growth. We will discuss ways to see your own future positively, seek out meaningful goals, and honor your progress without demanding perfection. The chapter also outlines how to stay hopeful when setbacks arise, how to tap into sources of inspiration, and how to keep building a life that feels worth living. Hope is more than an emotion—it is a daily practice of believing you can continue moving forward.

Why Hope Matters

1. **Boosts Motivation**
    - Hope can give you energy to keep trying new actions, to wake up and do your morning routine, or to engage with friends. Without hope, you might ask, "What is the point?" Hope answers that your efforts can yield better moments.
2. **Counteracts Negative Thoughts**
    - Depression may say you have no future, but hope disputes that voice. Hope does not deny your challenges; it simply insists that improvement is still possible, however slowly it may arrive.

3. **Sparks Creativity**
    - When you feel that things can get better, you often look for new ideas and solutions. Hope opens your mind to different approaches you may not have noticed while feeling trapped.
4. **Helps You Face Failures**
    - Everybody fails at times. Hopeful people understand that a setback is not the end. They adapt and try again, trusting that the next attempt might bring better results.
5. **Fosters Connections**
    - When you show some level of hope, others may feel inspired to connect with you. People often want to be around those who have a hopeful spirit. This can form a positive cycle, further supporting your mental well-being.

Releasing Past Pain

1. **Accepting What Happened**
    - Hope for the future does not mean forgetting past hurts. It means acknowledging them as part of your history but not letting them rule your tomorrow. You can still grieve, but you do not have to live solely in sorrow.
2. **Letting Go of Blame**
    - If you keep blaming yourself for past mistakes, it is hard to imagine a better tomorrow. By practicing forgiveness (detailed in earlier chapters), you free mental space to consider positive changes ahead.
3. **Opening Up Your Narrative**
    - Your story is not locked. Even if you have seen yourself as someone who always struggles, you can add new chapters to your life story. That does not

erase the sad parts—it simply expands to include possibilities of light and growth.

4. **Learning from the Past**
   - Reflect on what your sadness has taught you about your needs, boundaries, or values. If you see that ignoring stress signals led you to a breakdown, that knowledge can guide you to do things differently going forward.
5. **Building Strength from Wounds**
   - Surviving dark times often makes you stronger in empathy or understanding. You may better grasp other people's pain or value small joys more. This sense of hard-earned wisdom can be part of your hope.

Imagining a Worthwhile Future

1. **Begin with Small Visions**
   - If looking far ahead feels overwhelming, imagine the next week or month. What do you want to accomplish or experience in that shorter span? Focusing on near-term goals can form a bridge to bigger dreams.
2. **Identify What You Enjoy**
   - Sometimes, depression steals your sense of pleasure. As you start feeling less weighed down, revisit what used to make you smile or pique your interest. List a few activities or topics that spark curiosity.
3. **Explore Possibilities**
   - You do not need to lock yourself into one life path. Hope can involve sampling new hobbies or studying a new subject. If you sense a small flicker of excitement, follow it a bit and see where it leads.
4. **Talk About the Future**

- Share with a trusted friend or family member about something you hope to do. Even if it is just wanting to learn a cooking technique or plan a low-key trip, voicing it makes it more real. They might offer ideas or join you.

5. **Update Goals Over Time**
    - Goals evolve. If you set a target (like building a consistent exercise habit) and meet it, you can create a fresh aim. Continuously refreshing goals keeps hope alive and guards against boredom.

Finding Inspiration

1. **Stories of Resilience**
    - Look for stories of people who overcame hardships—whether in books, articles, or short videos. These can remind you that others have walked through darkness and found light again.
2. **Role Models**
    - Think about someone you admire, maybe a teacher or someone in your family, who has faced difficulties and stayed optimistic. What attitudes did they show? How did they keep going?
3. **Art, Music, and Media**
    - Sometimes, a song or a painting can speak to your heart about hope more than an essay can. Engaging with art that resonates with you can lift your spirits, even briefly.
4. **Nature's Example**
    - Observing nature—like noticing how plants regrow after winter—can offer comfort that cycles exist. Day follows night; spring follows winter. This can be a gentle reminder that change is a normal part of life.
5. **Guidance from Counselors or Mentors**

- A professional or a mentor can share encouraging perspectives. They might have witnessed many stories of people who improved over time. Hearing such examples can strengthen your sense of hope.

Building a Sense of Purpose

1. **Discover What Gives You a Reason to Keep Going**
    - This might be caring for a pet, wanting to support a sibling, or a simple desire to see a new season of a favorite show. No reason is too small if it helps you hold on.
2. **Look for Acts of Kindness**
    - When you help someone else, you often feel a sense of meaning. That might be volunteering once a month, being a good listener to a friend, or creating something that brings joy to others.
3. **Reflect on Personal Values**
    - Consider what principles matter to you—kindness, honesty, creativity, loyalty. Aligning your actions with these values can provide a sense of direction and hope, even on difficult days.
4. **Taking on Gradual Challenges**
    - Sometimes, tackling a new skill or small project gives you a sense of worth. These do not need to be monumental tasks. Even learning to bake a simple bread can feel like an achievement when you complete it.

Holding Onto Hope During Struggles

1. **Practical Hope vs. Blind Optimism**

- Practical hope recognizes real problems but insists that solutions or improvements are possible. Blind optimism might ignore the difficulties altogether, which can lead to frustration when reality hits. Aim for a balanced viewpoint.

2. **Micro-Hopes**
    - If you cannot imagine big changes, look for tiny sparks: "Maybe tomorrow I will feel a bit lighter," or "I can get through this task, then rest." These small hopes can be stepping stones.
3. **Accept Feelings Without Abandoning Hope**
    - You can hold two truths: "I feel sad or anxious right now" and "I still believe I can get through this." Emotions are not permanent states; they can shift over time.
4. **Lean on Your Support Network**
    - In times of slipping hope, reach out to those who can remind you of your progress or capabilities. Sometimes an outside voice can see your strengths better than you can in a low moment.
5. **Remember Past Victories**
    - Recall times you overcame problems before. If you handled stress in the past, you can do so again. This memory helps you realize you have overcome or managed big issues before, which can stir hope.

Creating a Vision Board or Notebook

1. **Collect Meaningful Images and Words**
    - You can cut pictures from magazines or print out quotes that resonate with you. Arrange them on a poster or in a notebook. Include uplifting phrases that remind you of your reasons to keep going.
2. **Keep It Visible**

- Place it where you see it often—on a desk or a wall. On tough days, it can serve as a silent encouragement. A quick glance might spark a tiny smile or a moment of motivation.
3. **Update It Over Time**
    - As your interests or goals change, add fresh clippings or remove things that no longer inspire you. Keeping it dynamic ensures it reflects your current hopes.
4. **Not a Cure-All**
    - A vision board or notebook is not magic, but it can provide a gentle daily reminder that you have positive aims and values in mind.
5. **Reflect on Each Image**
    - When you have time, pause at an image and ask, "What does this represent? Why did it speak to me?" This reflection can deepen your emotional connection to your hopes.

Balancing Hope with Realism

1. **Recognize Real Obstacles**
    - Hope does not mean pretending everything is perfect. You might have real limits, like financial constraints or health challenges. Embracing hope means seeking ways around or through these barriers, not ignoring them.
2. *Celebrate Steps, Not Only End Results**
    - If your goal is to gradually regain physical fitness, each time you do a short walk is worth acknowledging. Waiting only to feel good when you reach the final outcome can cause you to miss the positive moments along the way.
3. **Use Setbacks as Data**

- If something fails or goes poorly, see it as information. Ask yourself what you can learn from it. This approach helps you stay hopeful by transforming failure into an opportunity to refine your path.
4. **Accept That Some Things Take Time**
    - Growth in relationships, career, or personal health might unfold over months or years. Holding onto hope for the long term means trusting in slow progress, even if day-to-day changes are subtle.
5. **Plan B or C**
    - Sometimes, you might need alternative strategies if your main plan hits a roadblock. Keeping a backup plan reminds you that there are still options when the first path does not work out.

Sharing Hope with Others

1. **Reach Out in Small Ways**
    - You do not have to be a motivational speaker. Simply sending an encouraging message to a friend who is down can spread a spark of hope to them. Being there for someone else can also solidify your own hope.
2. **Group Support**
    - Joining or forming a small group (online or in person) where you talk about what lifts you can help everyone. Hearing various viewpoints on staying hopeful can expand your own ideas.
3. **Being an Example**
    - If people notice you handling tough days with steady effort (not perfection), they might ask how you stay motivated. Sharing your coping methods can inspire them while reinforcing your commitment to those methods.
4. **Stay Clear of Toxic Positivity**

- Telling someone, "Just cheer up" or "It will be fine, stop worrying" can invalidate their feelings. Offering hope means listening, acknowledging their struggle, and gently suggesting that better moments can still arise.

5. **Highlight Real Stories**
   - If a friend is feeling hopeless, you could carefully share about a time you felt down but found a way through. Keep it authentic and not over-simplified. This personal proof can make hope feel more credible.

Embracing the Ongoing Nature of Hope

1. **Hope Evolves with You**
   - Today's hope might focus on regaining stability. Tomorrow's hope might shift toward exploring new opportunities. Allow your sense of hope to change as your life changes.
2. **Hope Is Not Constant Joy**
   - You can still feel sadness on certain days while holding hope. Hope sits beside difficult emotions, reminding you that sadness does not define your entire future.
3. **Practice, Practice**
   - Hope is a skill. You practice it by seeking positives, setting goals, reaching out for help, and reminding yourself of possibility when negative thoughts arise.
4. **Avoid Perfectionistic Thinking**
   - Expecting never to feel low again can lead to disappointment. Instead, be gentle with yourself. Aim for gradual progress, not total avoidance of all pain.
5. **Seek Professional Help if Hope Feels Gone**
   - If you cannot find a glimmer of hope at all, contact a counselor or mental health hotline. Sometimes you need outside support to rebuild that sense of

possibility. That is a normal step in the healing process.

Painting a Brighter Tomorrow

1. **Create a Personal Mantra**
   - A short phrase like, "I am open to better days," or "I have worth, and I can keep growing." Silently repeat it when negative thoughts intrude.
2. **Imagine Life a Year from Now**
   - Picture yourself a year into practicing supportive habits. Maybe you feel stronger, have new interests, or enjoy deeper relationships. This visualization can be a gentle push to continue your efforts.
3. **Note the Good in Each Day**
   - Even on rough days, there can be a decent moment: a small laugh, a calm breeze, or a kind gesture from someone. Write these down or think about them at bedtime. Such moments remind you that not all is dark.
4. **Plan Simple Adventures**
   - You do not need to do something huge. A short trip to a nearby park or museum can spark fresh appreciation for life's variety. Engaging in the world outside your usual bubble can gently stir a sense of hope.
5. **Stay Open to Surprises**
   - Sometimes, good things come unexpectedly—an old friend reaches out, or you discover a new talent. By staying open to these surprises, you remain flexible to the idea that life can hold pleasant changes.

Conclusion: A Continuing Path

Hope for the future does not guarantee that everything will be easy. You may still face stress, sadness, or tough situations. But hope plants a seed in your mind that says, "I can face these challenges and still find meaningful and bright moments ahead." Holding onto hope is not about denying pain; rather, it is about refusing to give pain the final say.

As you close this book, remember that you have gathered many tools. You learned about forming healthier routines, managing negative thoughts, building supportive bonds, checking your progress, and keeping steady gains. Now you add hope as a vital piece that weaves these elements together. Each day, in small ways, you can practice self-care, reach for supportive connections, and remain open to the possibility of positive change.

Your future—like everyone's—holds unknown twists. However, by continuing to apply what you have learned and by carrying a hopeful outlook, you can face new trials with resilience. Remember that you do not have to do it all alone. Your friends, family, counselors, or online communities can help. You can also help others, sharing your lessons and warmth. May you find comfort in the fact that depression, while powerful, does not own your story. With self-kindness, awareness, and a spark of hope, you can keep shaping each chapter of your life toward greater well-being.

In closing, always keep in mind that small steps do count. Every effort to take care of yourself, to speak kindly to your mind, to seek joy in tiny moments, and to share a caring word with someone else is building a foundation for a brighter view of tomorrow. Hoping does not mean ignoring difficulties; it means lighting a candle against the darkness. That candle—your hope—can guide you on days you feel lost and brighten your path forward. You have worth, your life has meaning, and you hold the power to keep growing in ways that support your mental health for years to come.

www.ingramcontent.com/pod-product-compliance
Lightning Source LLC
LaVergne TN
LVHW012042070526
838202LV00056B/5571